Signs of Our Past

Porcelain Enamel Advertising in America

Michael Bruner

4880 Lower Valley Road, Atglen, Pa 19310

Schiffer Books are available at special discounts for bulk purchases for sales promotions or premiums. Special editions, including personalized covers, corporate imprints, and excerpts can be created in large quantities for special needs. For more information contact the publisher:

Published by Schiffer Publishing Ltd.
4880 Lower Valley Road
Atglen, PA 19310
Phone: (610) 593-1777; Fax: (610) 593-2002
E-mail: Info@schifferbooks.com

For the largest selection of fine reference books on this and related subjects, please visit
our web site at:
www.schifferbooks.com
We are always looking for people to write books on new and related subjects. If you have
an idea for a book please contact us at the above address.

This book may be purchased from the publisher.
Include $5.00 for shipping.
Please try your bookstore first.
You may write for a free catalog.

In Europe, Schiffer books are distributed by
Bushwood Books
6 Marksbury Ave.
Kew Gardens
Surrey TW9 4JF England
Phone: 44 (0) 20 8392-8585; Fax: 44 (0) 20 8392-9876
E-mail: info@bushwoodbooks.co.uk
Website: www.bushwoodbooks.co.uk
Free postage in the U.K., Europe; air mail at cost.

Dedication

To Heather Lynn Abbott

September 26, 1986 – August 20, 2005

*Your Love of God's Creatures has endeared our hearts.
May your soul be forever with God.*

Requiescat in pace.

Acknowledgements

As with any worthwhile endeavor, certain key people have made a lot of difference in how smoothly this book went together. The enthusiasm that was extended towards myself and this project in general have given me the ability to take this book's beginning ideas all the way to a published volume. I'd like to especially thank the following people for going the extra mile in contributing their special talents towards this book on North American porcelain enamel advertising.

To Peter Schiffer, my publisher, my sincere appreciation for your support and understanding when things got a little behind schedule.

To Sue Gladden, for coordinating the photo shoots for many of the southern California collectors.

To Sharon Callender, for her professional assistance with text layout, digital transcription, and of course, all the last-minute additions.

To Heidi Abbott, for her tolerance and perseverance with my globetrotting travels, and her assistance at many of the photo shoots, which made the work proceed in a timely manner.

To Mick and Christine Hoover, for their continued friendship and the ability to laugh when they were told that none of the photos came out from our original two-day session, due to my failure to check a particular switch on my camera.

To Jeff Kaye, who through the pages of this book shared his love of collecting porcelain enamel advertising, and sadly, has passed away — your friendship and intense interest in this hobby set an example for all. You are missed. God rest your soul.

To John Bobroff, for putting me up and putting up with me. Your beautiful mountain home is an oasis of porcelain enamel.

To Bob Newman, for allowing the collecting world to see your beautiful acquisitions, which is nothing short of the finest country store porcelain enamel sign collection in the country. Your help and advice on values is much appreciated.

To Christopher Baglee and Andrew Morley, the true pioneers of porcelain enamel advertising research and collecting — you are the porcelain enamel world's mentors. Thanks from all of us on both sides of the Atlantic.

And, finally, to all my contributors, it was so rewarding to meet with you and photograph your collections. My heartfelt thanks to each of you. It is you that have made this book a reality. — *Michael Bruner*

Contributors

The following is a listing of contributors who have shared their time and allowed me to photograph items from their collections. Some individuals wish to remain anonymous, and their contributions, although not acknowledged here, are much appreciated.

Bob Mewes, Winona, Texas; John Collins, Mt. Vernon, Illinois; Pete Keim, Sunnyvale, California; Dick Marrah, Penryn, California; Butch Grier, Magnum, Oklahoma; Gas Pump Ronnie, Hesperia, California; Kramer Antiques and Pottery, Boron, California; Pam and Jon Pomeroy, Covena, California; Long Beach Antique and Collectibles Mall, Long Beach, California; Dennis and Jeanne Weber, St. Joseph, Missouri; Rick and Pamela Stevens, Southgate, Michigan; Greg Stevens, Southgate, Michigan; Mike Mihkelson, Long Beach, California; Jeff Kaye, Yucca Valley, California; Bob Newman, Encino, California; Dennis Griffin, Orange, California; Sue Gladden, Laverne, California; Rod and Sandy Krupka, Ortonville, Michigan; John Bobroff, Running Springs, California; Mick and Christine Hoover, Mackay, Idaho; Dick and Diane Kinsey, Modesto, California; Bill Rohde, Williams, California; Darryl Fritsche, Hesperia, California

Contents

Preface

A lot has been happening since my previous editions of *The Encyclopedia of Porcelain Enamel Advertising*. Most significant is the role that the Internet has played in the marketplace. This has been a boon to buyers and sellers, as it has provided the tools to educate people about the true scarcity of many signs. The past few years have seen a tremendous growth in collecting antique advertising. Of the many media used by companies to bring attention to their products or services, none seem to have had the overall appeal of porcelain enamel. The process of creating porcelain signs is actually an art in itself, and the influx of new collectors in the market place attests to porcelain enamel advertising's beauty. Few collectibles are made with such long-lasting properties or have been found in such diversity as porcelain enamel advertising.

For all the magnificent designs that have turned up through the years, it is interesting to note that the hobby of collecting this advertising is of relatively recent vintage. Possibly collectors couldn't see the forest for the trees! So many times we have been bombarded with advertising in our everyday life that we really paid little attention to such matter-of-fact items. I've been to many places that had some type of porcelain sign outside the building, only to find out the owner had no idea that the advertising sign I mentioned was on the premises!

Like so many other collectibles, the stimulus for collecting porcelain enamel advertising is that it's no longer being manufactured, and it is quickly disappearing from the eye of the general public. The past few years have seen the removal of most of the remaining porcelain enamel signs that were still "in use." Normally, a long search will not turn up anything but the most common or mundane pieces doing service. With little porcelain advertising to be found in its original place, those wanting a piece of the action must now turn to the collector's market to acquire these artifacts.

The heartbeat of any hobby is the ability to buy, sell, or trade. Collecting porcelain advertising is certainly no different in that it is the people in the hobby that make it an enjoyable experience. It is possible to build a fine collection by staying at home, going on the Internet, writing letters, and making phone calls. However, to really network yourself, it pays to get out to the trade shows. Many dealers are specialists in advertising, and come up with some pretty unusual items. A few shows throughout the country even specialize in advertising, and a good mix of porcelain advertising usually will be present. These shows are generally well advertised in the major antique pub-

lications. Don't get discouraged by the fact that some of the pieces you want for your collection are not available. Patience will almost always pay off in the long run. And as far as prices go, if you like it and you can afford it, then buy it! I've been involved in several hobbies through the years, and in my judgment collecting porcelain advertising will continue to go through the roof in future years. Not every sign will be a breadwinner, but on the average most advertising does appreciate in value over time. This is especially true on the better items.

As you go through this book, you'll notice the tremendous degree of diversity found in porcelain advertising. Not only signs, but also dozens of other everyday items were made with a porcelain message. Keep in mind that you are looking only at the tip of the iceberg. There were thousands of porcelain signs manufactured in this country during the last hundred-plus years. However, due to World War IIs scrap effort, possibly as few as thirty percent of the total signs manufactured have survived. Despite this seemingly discouraging view, there are endless possibilities to acquire these historical artifacts on the Internet alone. And for those of you that are adventuresome, a little perseverance will reward you with new finds in basements, attics, bulk plants, and defunct manufacturing facilities. Proof of this can be seen at antique advertising shows, with a never-ending stream of new discoveries coming through the door.

I'd like to make special mention of the fact that we in America are not alone in our interest in collecting porcelain enamel advertising. As a matter of fact, it has been going on worldwide for years. I have had the pleasure of meeting with collectors in Europe and they share the same objectives as us here in America: to preserve these historical items. England in particular has been a mecca for collectors, as they have been blessed with the most graphic advertising you could ever imagine. This is due in part to the European artisans in the 1800s that were laying down the framework for these early advertisements. Eventually, some of these English/European manufacturers found their way to the American marketplace, as the demand for high-quality artwork on porcelain could only be accomplished by calling on these supplemental overseas suppliers.

There is a huge collector following in England, due in large part to the early efforts of Christopher Baglee and Andrew Morley. These two pioneers were doing this stuff decades ago, and they were the first to publish a comprehensive guidebook on the subject aptly titled, *Street Jew-*

elry. Their most recently published 240-page hardbound edition is a work of art in itself, and is nothing short of an amazing assortment of rare advertising throughout the world. Congratulations to both of you on this accomplishment. You make me look like a beginner! You can order the book or join the Street Jewelry Society, a worldwide porcelain enamel advertising collectors' group by email at: *streetjewelry@andrewmorley.com.*

So sit back, grab a drink, and enjoy this amazing tour through time. I'm sure you will find that it will give you an idea of the beauty and diverse graphics that can be found in this very collectible area of Americana.

I look forward to hearing from you. Please feel free to write me c/o 6576 Balmoral Terrace, Clarkston, MI 48346. — *Michael Bruner*

Introduction

To better understand how porcelain enamel advertising came into collectible status, a brief review of its day-to-day use is helpful. As the art of porcelain enamel production was perfected, it became an inexpensive way for a business to promote its products. Shortly after the turn of the twentieth century, porcelain enamel advertising became so commonplace that few merchants could be found without some type of porcelain sign being displayed. No longer was porcelain advertising a luxury. It became the standard by which to judge all other advertising forms.

As the years progressed, so did the imaginations of those responsible for creating this medium. Square and rectangular signs gave way to extravagant "die-cut" designs. New effort was put into the color schemes. Anything and everything was tried on porcelain enamel. As a result, manufacturers were kept busy for the better part of the twentieth century.

In time, though, many manufacturers went by the wayside. The smaller ones could not compete, and the rising costs involved in the production of porcelain enamel made many businesses consider alternative methods of advertising. This spelled doom for the porcelain enamel sign manufacturers. By the 1970s, with the exception of some municipal and sundry signs, the production of porcelain enamel advertising became a closed chapter in American history.

The good news is that collectors have recognized porcelain enamel as a historical connection to the past. It is a link to the products and services that made this country great. Unfortunately, most of the companies that advertised in porcelain are no longer with us, but some are still around, possibly due to the manufacturer identification marks they used throughout the years.

The products to be found advertised in porcelain are almost endless. As you read through the book, you will see the wide range of advertisers who used this medium. There seem to be certain subjects that received more of the advertising market than others, particularly the products or services that were frequently used by the public. Leading the list would be petroleum signs, and any advertising relating to the automobile or gasoline. It would be safe to say that more petroleum-related porceiain enamel advertising was produced than in any other

category. Many collectors specialize in "petro" advertising and find the number of items produced over the years nearly endless. Other companies that made heavy use of porcelain advertising were manufacturers of beer, paints and varnishes, telephone, tobacco, and soda pop.

As a collector, don't make the mistake of trying to acquire everything. If you want to collect by the pound, that is fine; but keep in mind how much is out there! It's just not practical to think that you can collect everything that was produced. Instead, set your sights on a more realistic approach. One of the most common would be to specialize in a certain company or product. One collector I know collects only blue and white porcelain, and he says it goes great with his graniteware! Possibly a special interest in your personal life will find its way to your collection. For instance, I know several people who are telephone company employees that specialize in porcelain telephone advertising. After a brief period you will find out what it is that interests you.

You will find this book divided into several chapters. Each chapter covers items by manufacturing design, or subject matter. Each photograph will have a brief description and any relevant comments. This will be followed by the item's measurements — height first, then width. The approximate age of the sign will also be given. Please keep in mind that estimating the age of a sign is done through a combination of several techniques, which are covered in a separate section in the book. There is a glossary of commonly used nomenclature for collectors near the back of the book. Pay attention to the definitions, as they will help you communicate effectively in the hobby.

For those of you privileged enough to have lived in the era of porcelain advertising, get ready for a trip down memory lane. And for those of us wishing to go back to a time we never saw, the following pages will provide a vivid portrait of our past in porcelain enamel advertising.

A Sign's History

Estimating A Sign's Age

Very few porcelain signs have been made with the date of manufacture or their intended location marked on them. The most notable exception to this would be some of the Coca-Cola signs that had their manufacture date ink stamped on them. Most of these date to the 1930s. Some automobile signs have been found with the year of their service on them as well. For the most part, though, a sign's age cannot be pinpointed without a date right on the sign. There are, however, some techniques that can be helpful in determining a sign's approximate age.

The most scholastic method requires the name of the manufacturer to be on the sign. If this information is known, then some research can tell you the dates that the company was in business. This may not in itself accomplish much, because many companies were producing signs for decades. If the street address of the manufacturer is on the sign you might get a better idea of a sign's age, because many times a company's operations at a particular address were for only a brief time. These methods take some real knowledge of the companies that were in business, and you might spend considerable time researching this information.

Another approach would be to "size up" the product advertised. This means that if you know the history of the product or service that is advertised on the sign, you can use this information to help you determine the sign's age. For example, if you found a "Mobil Gas" sign with the "Pegasus" logo on it, you would know that the sign was later than the 1920s. Mobil did not use the Pegasus logo until the 1930s. Similarly, if you guessed that a Brazil Beer sign dates in the 1940s, you would be considerably off, as this company was doing business only during the first years of the twentieth century.

Although these methods are helpful, using them requires knowledge of the products being advertised. There is another method that seems to work even better. The most accepted and reliable method of dating a sign is the look and feel of the porcelain. Most of the older signs – those dating before 1930 – were made using a stencil. This technique always produced a "bumpy" feel at the edges where different colors meet. Called "shelving," it was caused by the firing of more than one coat of porcelain. Some signs were fired five or six times, leaving the effect of shelving quite pronounced. Normally a sign made after 1940 will not have a high degree of this layered feel.

I must at this point temper my comments with the added caveat that a fair amount of reproduction and fantasy items have entered the marketplace. This has been going on for over thirty years, but the last few years especially have seen a healthy proliferation of new advertising being manufactured. Unfortunately, most all of these items are not marked as such, leaving it up to the buyer to determine what is original, and what is not.

The most significant fakes to surface are some signs produced around 1990 that can fool even seasoned collectors. They were made using the same techniques as signs produced one hundred years ago. I have plenty of experience with identifying these pieces, but the casual collector will not be aware of their recent lineage.

I know most dealers would not think of misrepresenting a new sign as being old, but my experience has been that you need to educate yourself about porcelain enamel dating techniques, because most signs will be sold with no guarantee. One of the drawbacks of good photography is that there is a fair amount of reproduction signs being made that were manufactured illegally by using copyrighted images from my previous books. Now that's low!

As unusual as this may seem, the backside of a sign may tell you more than the front. A porcelain coat will normally be found on the backside. The color of this coating can range from a light gray to a bluish-black and everything in between. The oldest signs will have many small "spots" where there is no porcelain. Some signs may have over a hundred of these small spots. This would indicate a sign of pre-1930 vintage, as manufacturers used methods that eliminated most of these spots after that time. This dating technique is for signs with the advertising on only one side.

A high degree of hand production work is also evident on older signs. It is common to find fingerprints fired right into the porcelain, sometimes in two or more colors! Once in a while you will find a set of numbers finger-written and fired into the porcelain. Let's say, for example, that you find the number "3-07." You could assume that the sign in your hands was manufactured in March of 1907!

As you gain experience as a collector, you will find your ability for estimating a sign's age has improved. Talking with other collectors is helpful. You can learn quickly from their knowledge.

Grading Condition

The increased use of the Internet, mail, and telephone for buying and selling antique advertising has created a need to develop a standard grading scale. Condition on a piece is of extreme importance when buying a sign "sight unseen." In the past there have been some problems in grading.

In describing a sign the seller must make an accurate assessment of damage. The buyer expects to have no surprises when the sign arrives, and if it has been graded correctly the buyer will be inclined to follow through with the transaction.

The majority of signs in "collectible" condition will fall into the grading scale between a rating of six and ten. Those pieces that are below grade 6.0 have lost enough of their eye appeal to be of limited interest. To get a more accurate guide to condition a value can be expressed in decimal points. As an example, to grade a sign between an eight and nine we would grade it an "8.5." This appears to be a universally accepted system of grading and offers better understanding than using terms such as mint, near mint, and very good.

The following descriptions should help you grade porcelain enamel signs:

Grade 10: Like new, out-of-the-box condition. Eyelets, if any, can show use or be missing, but no chips can be around the eyelet holes or anywhere else on the sign.

Grade 9.5: Very close to like-new condition with original luster to the porcelain but with a slight amount of damage, such as small screw hole chips, light scratches, or a small chip to non-critical sections of the image area. Small edge nicks in limited numbers could also be found.

Grade 9.0: Small areas of edge damage that do not detract from the overall appearance of the advertising. Several small or one larger edge chip is acceptable. Porcelain gloss should be intact, but the surface may show slight signs of use. The image area may have a small chip.

Grade 8.5: Chips become more numerous or may go into some of the image area. There may be slight loss of luster to part of the porcelain. Edge damage becomes more prominent, but does not detract from the overall appearance.

Grade 8.0: The image area may have a small amount of damage that will detract somewhat, but this will be confined to a minimum. There can be surface scratches or loss of luster. Damage outside the image area is more pronounced, with many edge chips or larger-sized chips to the screw holes or the flange area.

Grade 7.5: More noticeable damage to the sign with several larger-sized chips. The porcelain may have loss of luster in some areas and surface scratches could detract somewhat. Chips in the image area will be present, but will not be so large that a significant amount of eye appeal is lost. Flange damage could be extensive.

Grade 7.0: Chipping is more pronounced, with many edge chips and several more in the image area. There may be chips in a critical area of the image. Much wear could be present with scratching and significant loss of porcelain luster.

Grade 6.0: There is significant loss of eye appeal, with the image area damaged considerably. Several larger-sized chips will be present, and flange damage could be severe.

Grade below 6.0: Anything lower than 6.0 is missing a great amount of eye appeal, most likely from the significant loss of porcelain. These signs are just "fillers" until a better specimen makes its way to you.

Keep in mind that on flanged signs and signs that have an image area on both sides, a grade must be established for each side. Manufacturer defects will occasionally be present and although they are not considered damage, they should be mentioned.

As a rule, all chips are not created equal! Edge chips are not as significant as the same-sized chips on the inside area. Normally the edge area can expect to have some damage, and this is not as critical as the center being damaged. The principal question to answer is how much the damage detracts from the appeal of the sign. A 30" Conoco minuteman sign in super condition, except that a chip the size of a quarter "took out" the minuteman's face, will go from a condition of 9.5 plus to around 7.0 simply because few collectors would find a faceless minuteman very attractive. This is especially true at the prices these signs are going for!

As noted above, if the sign has a flange, a mention of the condition should be made, keeping in mind that flange damage is not as critical to a sign's appeal as damage to the face.

As you and other collectors "network" with those who share similar interests, it will pay to be as honest and accurate as possible in grading the condition of signs.

Restorations

Pricing

The last few years has seen a change in the collectors' market relative to porcelain enamel restoration. Many collectors who had been somewhat opposed to this approach have changed their tune. This is especially true with the more advanced collectors. And why not?! The first thing a car collector does is rip off the rusty fenders and get out the bondo, this being done to show off the vehicle in like-new condition. Along with the added increase in monetary value, it just makes good sense and good business. Signs are no different. As prices continue to increase in the market, repairing a sign is a good decision, but you need to first contact the right person for the job. To do professional work requires much practice, and work of truly high quality comes from only a select few craftspeople.

When a sign that was damaged enough to be rated a seven is repaired so that it appears to be in mint condition, then you have a quality repair. There are people who can do repairs of this level, but you may not want to make the investment unless it will enhance the sign's value.

If you have a sign that has a market value of $300 in mint condition and the repair costs are $275, it might be in your best interest to leave it and invest in a more worthwhile repair. Normally, the higher-priced signs will be worth the cost of repairs, again provided the workmanship is high caliber.

How does a repair affect the value of a sign? There are some variables to consider, including the extent of repair on the sign and the quality of the work. On average, though, a sign that had a quality repair job would be worth at least seventy-five percent of what the sign would have been worth in mint condition with no repairs. For example, if a given sign has a market value in mint condition of $1,000, then a sign that's repaired so that it appears to be in mint condition should be worth at least $750. Again, it must be emphasized that these figures are for quality repairs only. Home-type "garage" repairs most likely will do little to enhance a sign's value, and may even lower it!

The decision to repair a sign is solely that of the sign's owner. Just like with antique cars, I personally feel that collectors have an obligation to preserve these artifacts for future generations. Terry and Dawn Hubert, of 2660 Greg Avenue, Brighton, MI 48114, do excellent, quality repairs. They can also be reached at 810-225-1886.

The values given in this book are fairly accurate market prices at the time of printing. They are for the actual signs that are in the photographs and reflect condition as seen. When trying to determine the value of a sign such factors as graphics, condition, subject matter, rarity, desirability, regional economy, the mood of the seller, phases of the moon, and a dozen other variables may come into play. Don't hold these prices as gospel; rather, temper them with your experience and knowledge.

Chapter One:
Flat One-Sided Signs

The signs in this chapter were all manufactured with the advertising on one side only. You will notice that the placement of mounting holes changes from one sign to the next. Each design called for a different support method. Most of the signs seen here will be for mounting to a wall. Some could be used in other situations such as fastening to a cart or a cooler. Others were designed to be mounted on the sides of trucks. A few were made to fasten together with another of the same sign, back to back.

In the 1920s many states utilized directional signage to help motorists find their way to some of the more prominent points located near highways. My home state, Michigan, was one of them, except they were large affairs made entirely of wood, totally unlike the beautiful porcelain example presented here. The exact location where this sign was used unfortunately cannot be determined, as there are probably over one hundred Indian Lakes scattered across the United States. Even the beautiful graphic of the Indian isn't much help since all these type of directional signs used a similar Indian chief in full headdress. Not knowing its original intended location, though, certainly has not taken away from its wonderful eye appeal—this warrior is a keeper! It measures 22" x 46" and dates from the 1920s.
Courtesy of Bob Newman. $2,500

Porcelain signs were manufactured for some highway departments. As you may know, California was a big user of porcelain enamel municipal and highway signs. Although the wording is difficult to read at the bottom of this 78 State Highway sign, the bear logo gives this piece away as being from California. It measures 16" x 18" and dates from the 1930s.
Courtesy of Sue Gladden. $800

This generic advertisement could have been used by any highway department throughout the United States. It appears that it was manufactured to be placed in a framework with two identical signs being back-to-back, or placed in a square framework with four signs displayed. Of course, the central focus of this sign is the beautiful red touring sedan seen near the bottom. With images such as these, dating this sign becomes no problem. It measures 61" x 28" and obviously dates from the 1920s.
Courtesy of Mick Hoover. $1,600

A close-up examination of the touring sedan reveals its generic nature, but who's looking at such trivialities? Graphics like these are what collectors' dreams are made of.
Courtesy of Mick Hoover.

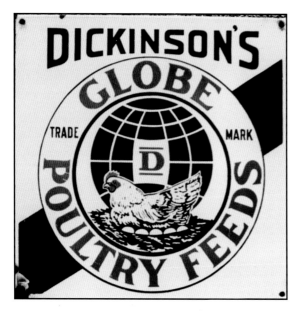

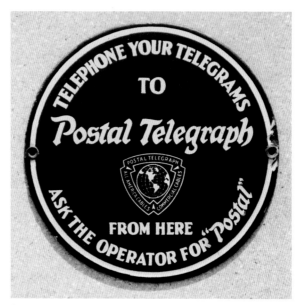

There were several different signs manufactured by Dickinson's over the years. Some featured a chicken lying on a nest of eggs, while others only had their logo at its center. Advertising relating to farming seems to have come into its own in recent years, as reflected in its demand and pricing. It measures 13.5" x 13" and dates to around 1930. *Courtesy of Bob Newman.* $850

When looking at this sign, you might be perplexed as to why you couldn't simply just telephone the person you were trying to reach instead of using an additional service provided by Postal Telegraph. Possibly the recipient had no telephone. Whatever the case, this 8" round sign was used sometime in the 1920s or 1930s. *Courtesy of Mick Hoover.* $300

At first glance this Kirschbraun & Sons Creamery sign seems to be an unremarkable example of an 18" x 15" advertisement. Upon closer examination, one may wonder what happened to the mounting hole on the right center of the sign and why the two right side grommet holes are offset. As the story goes, what is seen here is actually only 15" of a 6' long advertisement that had been cut off from the main part of the sign. Possibly the rest of the sign was so damaged that it made this the most attractive solution for salvation. At any rate, the milk can graphics are wonderful. *Courtesy of John Bobroff.* $400

The going rate for most cigars in the early 1900s was five cents. This Cressman's Counsellor sign shows their product being competitively priced. The wooden frame around the perimeter of the sign appears to be quite old and possibly done when the sign was originally installed. However, I won't go as far to say that this was done at the factory. Not readily seen in the photograph are the volcano screw holes, a popular sales feature that was patented by Ingram-Richardson. The sign measures 13" x 31" and most likely dates to around 1910. *Courtesy of Jeff Kaye.* $500

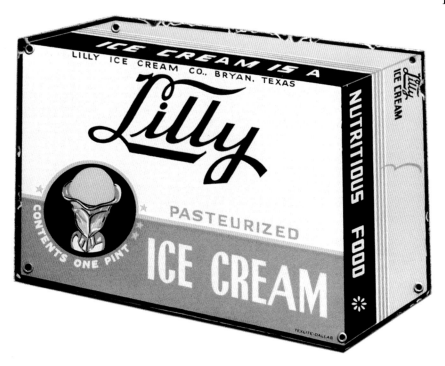

Bryan, Texas was home to Lilly Pasteurized Ice Cream. This multi-colored die-cut half-gallon container sign was manufactured by Texlite of Dallas, Texas, and measures approximately 17" x 12" inches. It dates to the 1930s. *Courtesy of Sue Gladden.* $1,200

This Salada Tea advertisement was used around 1930. Its die-cut shape represented the half-pound package that was used for their product. It measures approximately 5" x 15". *Courtesy of Bob Newman.* $900

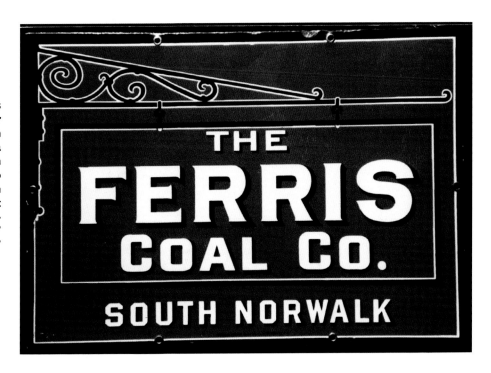

Ingram-Richardson manufactured this Ferris Coal Co. sign sometime prior to 1930. Occasionally, a porcelain sign can be found utilizing in its graphics a picture of an iron support bracket. Such is the case seen here. What appears to be damage on the left side of the sign is actually the silhouette of the bracket against the wall. Embossed "Ingram-Richardson, Beaver Falls, Pennsylvania" and "100 Williams Street, New York." Measures 14" x 20". *Courtesy of John Bobroff.* $250

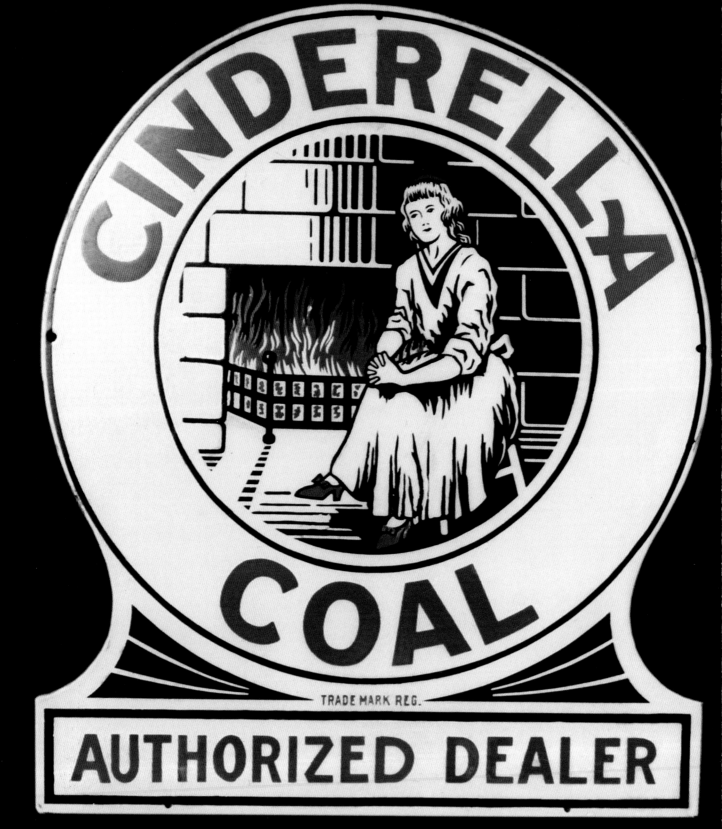

Cinderella appears to be patiently waiting for her prince to come along in this 1930s die-cut coal sign. Notice the nifty red slippers! Measures 26.5" x 18" and dates from the 1930s.
Courtesy of Dick Marrah. **$1,100**

In 1939 J. L. and Cal Turner opened a wholesale store in Scottsdale, Kentucky. In 1955 they named their store Dollar General with no item costing over one dollar. Today their annual revenue exceeds nine billion, possibly due in part to such catchy advertising as their image of a young man in uniform. Although newer, dating from around 1960, it certainly presents a lot of graphics and color. Of course, due to its age it was manufactured using a silkscreen. It measures 16" x 13.5". *Courtesy of Bob Newman. $350.*

Due to the optimal climate conditions, California has seen dozens of large-scale fruit growers throughout its history. Pure Gold was a trade name used by a conglomerate of growers under the name Mutual Orange Distributors. This 12" round advertisement appears to date from around 1940. *Courtesy of Rod Krupka. $400*

The reverse side of the Pure Gold Distributors sign shows a proprietary ink stamp. Sometimes I'm perplexed as to why they bothered, as the front side advertisement removes all doubt of ownership. *Courtesy of Rod Krupka.*

The side of an airport service vehicle or delivery truck could have possibly been uses for this 1950s Pan American World Airways sign. Trivial, but unusual, is the fact that there's only one center grommet hole at the bottom. Measures 18" x 24".
Courtesy of Bob Newman. **$500**

This American Quality Coal sign was intended to be placed on the side of a truck, made obvious with the words, "Orders Taken By Driver." It measures 9" x 12" and dates to around 1930.
Courtesy of John Bobroff. **$250**

Although it's not particularly scarce, the exceptional condition of this Model Smoking Tobacco sign makes it a standout. An identical sign with a yellow background was also manufactured. It measures 34" x 11" and dates to the 1930s.
Author's Collection. **$400**

It's too bad someone had to take a whack out of this Acorn Fence sign. Its huge acorn graphics combined with it being a California piece makes it quite collectible to those who desire western memorabilia. It measures a scant 8" x 6" and is an early one, dating to the 1920s.
Courtesy of Sue Gladden. **$300**

All of our soft drinks today are manufactured as premixed concoctions. Although this has been the norm for over seventy-five years, there was a time when the mixing was done at a soda fountain in front of the customer. This beautiful blue and white soda sign advertises such a process. You started simply with soda water that was carbonated and added whatever flavoring was available. The company who had this sign produced appears to have been in business in the 1800s, as evidenced by the very early techniques and graphics used on the sign. If that weren't enough, the woman sketched in her Sunday best in the bottom right corner will remove all doubt. Most companies would have preferred to advertise their product's name largely on their advertising. That's not the case on this piece, as the small circle below the word "soda" says "Miller's Fine Flavors." Measures 18" x 24" inches and dates to around 1900.
Courtesy of Pete Keim. **$800**

I couldn't resist showing you the reverse side of the Soda sign. The red that can be seen on the back is not fired-on porcelain, but someone's sloppy paint mess that was left for future generations to see. The numbers "1, 2, and 0" are fired on and could have several meanings, possibly an indication that the sign was manufactured January 2, 1900.
Courtesy of Pete Keim.

Something a little more unusual was on the table when this Metropolitan Coal Company sign was on the drawing board. Why they chose a flagpole with company flag, who knows, but collectors are satisfied. It measures 14" x 19" and looks to be from the 1930s.
Courtesy of John Bobroff. **$450**

This Tydol 30" round advertisement is unusual as the Ethyl logo is not accurate as far as its coloration. This is due to the fact that they used the same orange Tydol color instead of the proper yellow the Ethyl Corporation used. It's just one more example of cutting corners to save some money. Still, it's a beautiful example of a 1930s advertisement.
Courtesy of Bob Mewes. **$1,500**

POLARINE OIL AND GREASES
BEST FOR ALL MOTORS

One of the most successful early names in the oil business was Polarine. This three-color example with block letters is in exceptional condition, measuring approximately 40" x 12". It dates from the 1930s.
Courtesy of Mick Hoover.
$600

Norwalk Tire used this die-cut pressed advertisement in the 1920s. It measures 19" x 16".
Courtesy of Bob Newman. **$1,000**

As most everyone knows, Coca-Cola has continued to be one of the most prolific advertisers on the planet. Unfortunately, this sometimes makes pinpointing an advertisement's exact use difficult—as is the case with this 9.5" round Coca-Cola sign dating from around 1940. Could it have been used in conjunction with a larger point of purchase advertisement? The possibilities are almost endless.
Courtesy of Bob Newman. **$800**

Dr. Pepper used several similar designs between 1930 and 1960 to advertise their famous soft drink, and this one is another variance on their "Good For Life" theme. It measures only 8" x 21" and has been pinpointed to being manufactured in 1948. Ink stamped "McMath Axelrod Dallas 48."
Courtesy of Bob Newman.
$400

This nifty 10" round sign featuring the image of an Eskimo was part of a multi-piece display used on the sides of delivery trucks. This sign dates from around 1950 and is highly sought after by collectors. *Courtesy of Sue Gladden.* $600

Here's something seen few and far between. The gorgeous graphics of a medieval knight on horseback makes for a high impact point-of-sale advertisement. The trade name "invader" was used at many different brands of service stations. Therefore, this sign could have been used widely in any number of locations throughout America. However, its rarity indicates a rather small production run. It measures 28" x 20" and dates from the 1920s. *Courtesy of Dick Marrah.* $5,000

USE **INVADER** MOTOR OIL

Guaranteed 100% PURE PENNSYLVANIA OIL

PERMIT-151

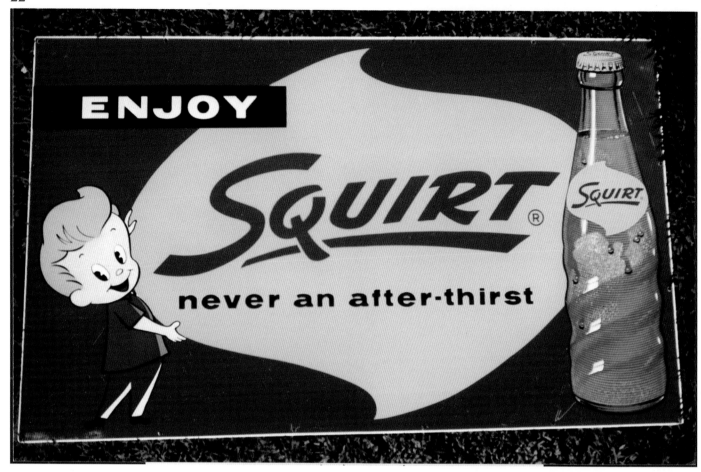

A popular citrus-flavored soda available throughout the country in the 1950s was Squirt. This simple but attractive sign was sure to produce sales. Measures 55" x 36". *Courtesy of Bob Newman.* $800

The ravages of time have eaten away, literally, at the bottom left corner of this Central Cottage Cheese sign. It may be hard to tell by the photograph, but this sign used extremely thick iron and porcelain enamel and wound up weighing quite a bit for its relatively small 7" x 20" size. *Courtesy of Jeff Kaye.* $300

A more recent vintage sign of localized origins would be this Wright's Pen Fed Beef sign. Probably manufactured in the 1950s, it measures a large 24" x 30" size. Notice the unusual blue shading that the manufacturer put in four locations around the perimeter. *Courtesy of Jeff Kaye.* $650

Overall advertising has been popular with collectors for many years. Though not a mainstream brand, Black Bear made an impression on the consumer with its graphic four-legged silhouette. Like many of the overall advertisements, this one is early, around 1915, and is ink stamped "Ingram-Richardson Beaver Falls PA." It measures 10" x 24". *Courtesy of Bob Newman.* $1,500

As one improves their collecting skills, little details become more noticeable. Such is the case on this White King Washing Machine Soap sign dating from around 1910. It's unusual for a manufacturer to be precise and put the writing upside down, as seen on this die-cut sign. I would think that readability would be paramount, but obviously correctness to box detail took front row seat. It measures 22" x 30". The White King Company was located in Los Angeles, California. *Courtesy of Jeff Kaye.* $2,200

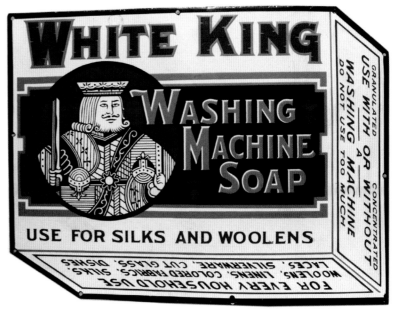

This banner style Gold Medal Flour sign dates from the 1920s. It measures 12" x 60" and is ink stamped with the "Burdick Consumers Building Chicago and Baltimore Enamel and Novelty Company Maryland" identification at the bottom right.
Courtesy of Rod Krupka. $750

Burdick of Chicago, Illinois, produced several variants on the three running devils with coal buckets for the Colorado Fuel & Iron Company. The one pictured here measures 9" x 20" and is ink stamped "Burdick Chicago" underneath the center grommet hole.
Courtesy of Mick Hoover. $550

It's unusual that the Old Mission Portland Cement Company didn't include its home town on this 14" x 14" cement sign. They were located in California. The sign dates to the 1930s.
Courtesy of Dick Marrah. $650

This die-cut coat of arms with a hooded knight is certainly an unusual piece. This was intended for use on a commercial unit of some type, as Kelvinator was a major trade name in the refrigeration business. It measures 12" x 10" and dates from the 1930s.
Courtesy of Bob Newman. $450

This small, 12" round A & W Root Beer sign was utilized in the 1950s and 1960s at their famous drive-in restaurants.
Private collection. $300

What a great item this is! One of the more unusual graphic signs is shown here with this Oswald Bros. Contractors example. It measures approximately 12" x 24" and shows the silhouette of a mule team pulling an early road grader. It dates to around 1920.
Courtesy of Mick Hoover. $1,500

Texlite was a porcelain enamel manufacturer located in Dallas, Texas. Their Texas lineage was proudly displayed in this porcelain sign featuring a sketch of the famous Alamo, which was an architectural style common in the American southwest. It appears this piece was intended to be a promotional giveaway as the two holes at the center bottom were designed to hold a calendar. Although those two holes and the one at the center top are original, the other four holes may have been someone's aftermarket handiwork. Notice the imitation wood porcelain finish that can occasionally be found on other porcelain advertisements as well. It measures 12" in diameter and dates to the 1930s.
Courtesy of Jeff Kaye. $400

Burdick of Chicago manufactured this "Danger" sign sometime in the 1920s. Somewhat of a minor detail, but nonetheless unusual, is the use of the larger grommet at the top. As it measures only 15" x 4.5", you would have to get fairly close to read this wordy little piece. *Courtesy of John Bobroff.* $150

KEEP AWAY
DANGER
WIRES HEAVILY
ELECTRIFIED
PRIVATE PROPERTY
REWARD for INFORMATION
LEADING TO THE ARREST
& CONVICTION OF ANY
PERSON WILLFULLY INJUR-
ING BUILDINGS, STRUCT-
URES, WIRES, INSULATORS,
TOWERS, POLES, SIGNS OR
ANY PROPERTY OF THIS
COMPANY.
YOUR REPORTING DE-
FECTS IN BUILDINGS,
STUCTURES AND WIRES,
BROKEN INSULATORS,
WASHED FOOTINGS, OR
ARCS ON LINES WILL BE
APPRECIATED.
WRITE, PHONE or WIRE COL-
LECT to any POWER HOUSE,
SUB-STATION or OFFICE of the
PENNSYLVANIA POWER &
LIGHT COMPANY OR TO
PENNSYLVANIA
POWER & LIGHT CO.
901 HAMILTON STREET
ALLENTOWN, PA.

Here's one from a long list of ice cream signs. This one appears to not have been used in the usual sidewalk stand, but rather would be placed on the side of a building—as evidenced by all the mounting holes around its perimeter. It measures 24" x 18" and is ink stamped at the bottom right "Baltimore Enamel 200 Fifth Avenue NY." *Courtesy of John Bobroff.* $400

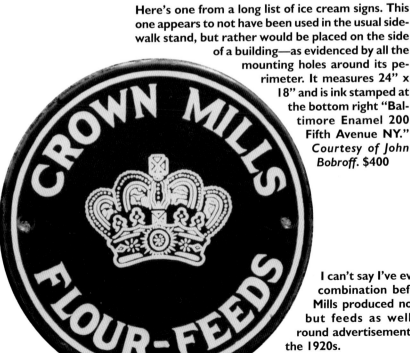

I can't say I've ever seen this combination before. Crown Mills produced not only flour but feeds as well. Their 6" round advertisement dates from the 1920s.
Courtesy of Dick and Diane Kinsey. $300

26

An otherwise mundane advertisement has been considerably spruced up with the addition of fruits, vegetables, and flowers. This sign dates from the 1940s and measures 18" x 28". *Courtesy of Mike Mihkelson.* $450

Although not particularly rare, this Lee Union-Alls advertisement gets the big bucks due to its great graphics featuring two workers in overalls. Both of the images were done by the decal process and are highly detailed. Dating from the 1920s, this wonderful advertisement measures 11" x 30". *Author's collection.* $2,400

Legitt's Creek Anthracite was one of many coal suppliers doing business in the 1920s. The rectangular advertisement seen here measures 12" x 30". *Courtesy of John Bobroff.* $500

Heating homes and commercial buildings with coal was big business until about the 1950s. This White Heat Coal and Coke sign measures 12" x 14". *Courtesy of John Bobroff.* $450

National Airlines utilized this 12" round porcelain sign around the 1940s. *Courtesy of Bob Newman.* $400

The 1920s saw production of this Lehigh Portland Cement sign. Notice the use of the saw tooth border, a familiar technique on advertisements in that time period. Upon closer examination, the word "office" can be seen in the red circle to the left near the bottom. They also produced a very similar sign, which I believe to be slightly later vintage, that had the Chicago, Illinois, regional office listed as well. And, one more tidbit: the barrel in the logo boasts of their company's yearly production being eight million barrels. That's a lot of cement. It measures 21.5" x 21.5". *Courtesy of Rod Krupka.* $500

This 8" x 15" die-cut Ruud Gas Water Heaters sign was most likely placed on their product. It's unusual that it has no mounting holes or bolts attached, leading one to believe that it may have been kept in place by some type of adhesive. It dates from around 1950. *Courtesy of Sue Gladden.* $150

Vesta was the goddess of the hearth in Roman mythology. This graphic sign with her image dates from the 1920s. It measures 12" x 20". *Author's collection.* $550

This small 4" x 7" sign was meant to be mounted on the front of a box containing telegraph cable blanks. This was obviously located in Canada and their system connected with Western Union's lines. It dates from the 1920s. *Courtesy of Mick Hoover.* $325

Prince Albert was one of the better-recognized tobacco trade names throughout the 1930s. This graphic rectangular example shows even the most illiterate person what they are advertising. Notice their interesting "national joy smoke" slogan. It measures 12" x 36" and dates to around the 1930s. *Courtesy of Rick and Pamela Stevens.* $1,875

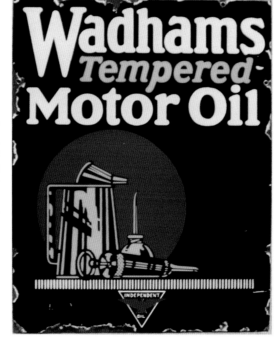

In the 1920s Wadhams Motor Oil was a recognized name in the field. This 20" x 16" sign is actually a rare variance on the more familiar two-sided-with-flange sign. *Courtesy of Mick Hoover.* $1,500

This large size Medusa Cement sign dates to the 1930s and measures 15" x 54". *Courtesy of Mick Hoover.* $525

Sharpless Ice Cream had this small-sized 5" x 7" sign produced for use on their freezers. Although the bottom right corner has the numbers "1904," it is highly unlikely this number is its manufacturing date as its manufacturing technique, along with its somewhat art deco-ness, would date this piece to more likely around 1930. Notice its similarity to the Hendlers Ice Cream sign found later in this chapter. Obviously they were both made by the same company. *Courtesy of Rick and Pamela Stevens.* $600

The company that manufactured Brower's Battery Brooders was most likely the source for this Fresh Tender Broilers sign to be given away when you purchased one of their Battery Brooders. It measures 18" x 28" and is from the 1920s. *Courtesy of Darrel Frish.* $350

No trespassing signs were an integral part of running an oil field for secure plant operation. Measures 8" x 24". *Courtesy of John Collins.* $1,000

These Department of the Interior Fish and Wildlife Service warning signs were placed on refuge areas throughout the United States. Although fairly common at one time, they are basically impossible to find nowadays and have become quite collectible. Each one measures 16" x 13" and dates to the 1950s. *Courtesy of Mick Hoover.* $600/pair

Across America thousands of independent oil wells helped supply America's thirst for crude. This Bishop Oil Company sign was on one such well and designated as leasee number 15. It measures 8" x 16" and dates to the 1940s. *Private collection.* $200

This three-piece Prescription Specialists sign is possibly a salesman's sample due to its scant 4" x 12" assembled size. The most likely end user for this piece would be Rexall, because of the well-known orange, blue, and white color scheme. It probably dates to the 1940s. *Courtesy of Mick Hoover.* $700

Boys and girls alike have grown up with that whimsical Red Goose Shoes logo. The 35" x 18" die-cut one pictured here is a pristine example dating from around 1930. *Courtesy of Bob Newman.* $1,700

The appropriate size for a sign on the side of a delivery truck is found in this 15" x 14" Providence Domestic Coke advertisement. Its two grommet holes in each corner suggests such a use. Providence Domestic Coke was located in Rhode Island and was doing business around 1930 when this sign was manufactured. It is ink stamped at the bottom, "Burdick Enamel Sign Company, Boston and Balto." *Courtesy of John Bobroff.* $350

This 4.5" x 4.5" Dririte Clothes Dryer sign no doubt was affixed to one of its products. *Courtesy of Mick Hoover.* $150

This die-cut Donberg Laundry Co. sign measures 4" x 4" and was probably used on some type of container. It dates to the 1920s. *Courtesy of Mick Hoover.* $100

The addition of a graphic ice cream cone and the five-cent price tag really helps bring an otherwise so-so sign to life. This multi-use advertisement could either be displayed on a wall or put back to back with an identical sign in a sidewalk-advertising stand. It measures 27" x 21" and is ink stamped at the bottom right "Baltimore Enamel 200 Fifth Avenue New York." It dates to around 1915. *Courtesy of Jeff Kaye.* $700

The 1940s saw the manufacture of this Eagle Green Stamp sign. Although the word "Green" with an arrow is pointing to a black and white stamp, financial considerations must have prevented them from using an additional color to produce a green stamp. It measures 15" x 36".
Courtesy of Rod Krupka. $500

By subject matter one would not think that cement signs could be very attractive. The dream-like graphic content of this Crescent Portland Cement Company sign makes it a standout! Any time I start to think I've seen it all, something like this turns up. The red spikes going around the perimeter have been used as an edge design on several other styles of porcelain advertising, most notably those of Adams Express, and have come to be known as a "saw tooth" border. This magnificent piece measures 15" in diameter and is early, dating to around 1910. *Author's collection.* $1,600

I'm not sure if this Fireman's Fund advertisement was to be placed curbside near the driveway of an agency's office building. Its small size could be readily overlooked. However, considering that it was produced in the 1920s, it must be remembered that automobile traffic was probably moving at less than thirty miles per hour at best. So my theory may not be too farfetched. It measures a scant 6" x 6". *Courtesy of Mick Hoover.* $400

Sunray Oils used this eight-sided advertising sign as their trademark logo. It measures 28" in diameter and dates from the 1930s. *Courtesy of Bob Mewes.* $1,800

34

This 12" round Navy League of the United States sign shows an anchor and banner with a prayer. It appears that its origin was from somewhere in Canada. It dates back to the 1950s.
Courtesy of Sue Gladden. $350

Another competitor in the motor oil market was Vico. It was important from their standpoint to get the message across that their product was made from 100% paraffin oil. The sign measures 34" x 26" and dates to sometime around 1930.
Courtesy of Dennis Griffin. $2,000

One of several with a fence theme, this Master Fence sign measures 5" x 8" and dates to around 1950.
Courtesy of Mick Hoover. $100

Southern Texas has similar climate to the region around Southern California. Similarly this Texsun Grower porcelain sign's function is like its Southern California counterpart, being used on farms that grew primarily fruit in the Southern Texas region near the Rio Grande River. Unusual is its scalloped border, which for some reason or another was rarely used on porcelain signs. It measures 14" in diameter and dates to around 1950.
Courtesy of John Bobroff. $350

Another of the many advertisements from citrus farms is seen on this Winter Haven Citrus Growers Association sign. It measures 11" square and is dated "1915" on its reverse side.
Courtesy of Bob Newman. $650

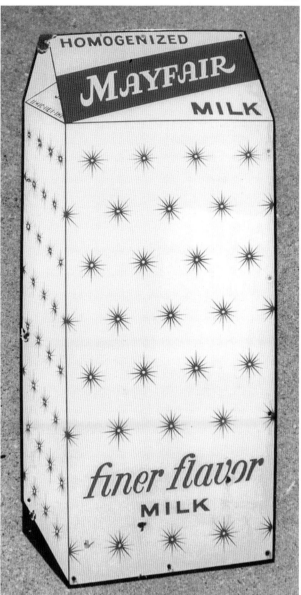

Milk container signs are popular with country store advertising collectors. This Mayfair Milk sign measures 34" x 16.5" and dates back to around 1940. They were located in New York.
Private collection. $250

Humphrey Radiantfire was an aftermarket stove-like product that could be used to convert your wood fireplace to an oil-burning heat source. This porcelain sign has a metal framework and was affixed to one of its products on a point of purchase display. It measures 8" x 21" and dates to the 1920s.
Courtesy of Darrel Fritsch. $300

The white and green cross has been the symbol of safety for many years. It is seen at the center of this Pittsburgh Coal Company sign that dates from the 1920s. It measures 10" x 12".
Courtesy of John Bobroff. $200

For years one of the largest manufacturers of canned tuna fish has been Star Kist. Their advertisement showing a large can of their well-known product is seen on this porcelain advertisement from the 1940s. It measures 18" x 20". *Author's collection.* $850

Porcelain was the material of choice when it came to long-lasting signage, as used by the United States Forest Service. There were literally hundreds of different forest directional signs to help back-road motorists, hikers, and hunters find

their way. The one shown here was located in southwestern Washington State. These signs have come into their own recently with newly kindled interest and subsequent prices in the marketplace. This example measures 4" x 12" and dates to around 1940. *Author's collection.* $200

Firemans Fund Insurance Co. of California used this 14" x 20" advertising sign sometime around 1925. The Brilliant Sign Company of Philadelphia, Pennsylvania, manufactured it. *Courtesy of John Bobroff.* $450

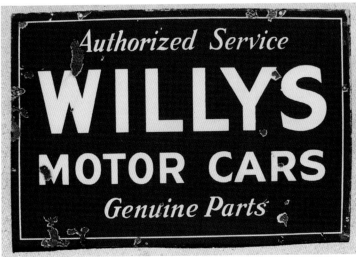

It amazes me that something like this exists. I am led to believe by the wording on this Airlec sign that garage doors will open by sounding your horn. Seeing that this advertisement dates to the 1920s, I had no idea that this kind of technology was available then. It measures 12" point to point. It is ink stamped "Nelke Signs, New York" at the bottom right. *Author's collection.* $450

This 1920s Willys Motor Cars Genuine Parts sign measures 24" x 36". *Private collection.* $750

It's likely that this Philip Morris strip sign was intended for mounting on doors. The twelve grommet holes highly suggest it was intended to be mounted that way. It measures 4" x 26" and dates to around 1930. *Courtesy of Rick and Pamela Stevens.* $700

A close-up of the Philip Morris cigarette pack shows how a fired-on decal can produce highly detailed images. This cigarette pack seems to take on a three-dimensional appearance. *Courtesy of Rick and Pamela Stevens.*

This smaller-sized Carnation Ice Cream sign measures approximately 10" x 10" and dates from the 1930s. *Courtesy of Bob Newman.* **$1,300**

Qualitee Dairy Products was located in San Diego, California. This 14" x 18" advertisement features a quart bottle of milk, adding greatly to the sign's collectivity. It dates to the 1930s. *Courtesy of John Bobroff.* **$600**

The unusual font and graphics used on this Solthern Ice sign suggests its location to be possibly in the southwest United States. The sign measures 16" x 48" and dates to around 1950. *Private collection.* **$250**

Here's an unusual piece. This 30" x 18" advertisement shows a large avocado. It dates to the 1930s. *Courtesy of Sue Gladden.* $250

This rare Sherwin-Williams Products porcelain sign was actually used as a clock face—as evidenced by the numbers around the green band. It measures 31" x 18" and dates from the 1920s. *Courtesy of Bob Newman.* $2,000

With the millions of pieces of glassware and china found in homes throughout America in the early part of the twentieth century, there arose a need to make repairs to broken pieces that were salvageable. This Major's Cement porcelain advertisement makes it clear what they were advertising. What's not so clear is the center graphics. It consists of a man's head drawn at the left, who presumably is Mr. Major, and a drawing of their packaging on the right. The center image is an award that was given at some prominent exposition and below that is a 200-pound weight suspended with hook and chain through one of the dishes that was repaired using Major's Cement, proving its strength and durability. This sign is an early one, dating to around 1910. It can be found in a similar-sized older version as well, with the center image a photographic decal fired onto the sign. It measures 6" x 24". *Courtesy of John Bobroff.* $350

A popular soft drink for many years has been Vernor's Ginger Ale. This early sign was used on the side of a dispenser. Notice that the top left and right corners of the sign have been notched out. This was done intentionally to accommodate the sign on the cooler and is not someone's aftermarket handiwork. *Courtesy of Mick Hoover. $700*

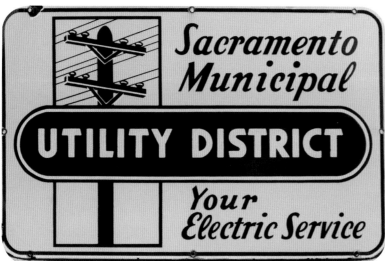

An electrical power substation was the likely target for this Sacramento Municipal Utility District sign. It measures 15" x 24" and dates from the 1950s. *Private collection. $400*

Apparently New York City had its share of toilet transients. This 1930s sign asks passengers to leave without unnecessary delay. After observing this sign, I'm not sure I would be willing to use these facilities in the first place. This warning was manufactured by L. D. Nelke Signs, New York, and is marked as such at the bottom right. It measures 10.5" x 19.5". *Courtesy of John Bobroff. $450*

"LOITERERS TAKE NOTICE"
PERSONS LOITERING IN THIS TOILET, OR MARKING THE WALLS OR DOORS, WILL BE ARRESTED & PROSECUTED.
PASSENGERS USING THE TOILET WILL PLEASE LEAVE WITHOUT UNNECESSARY DELAY.
INTERBOROUGH RAPID TRANSIT CO.

Black Magic Anthracite used this 14"
x 14" sign in the 1930s.
Courtesy of John Bobroff. $350

Many of the early security companies
had their own porcelain signs. By today's
standards, a $50 reward for the arrest and
conviction of a criminal seems paltry, but
when this sign was manufactured sometime
around 1920, that was a hefty amount. It
measures 10" x 14".
Courtesy of John Bobroff. $150

A surveyor's transit certainly is a
fitting symbol of the purpose behind
this Construction Engineers & Contractors sign. It measures 19" x 27"
and dates to around 1950.
Courtesy of Dick Marrah. $400

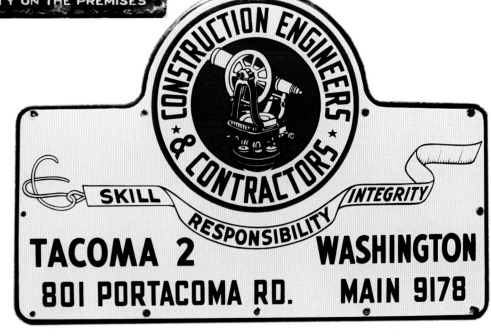

42

Another of the larger trade names in the tobacco industry was R. G. Sullivan. This 3" x
18" strip sign for their Dexter brand cigar was
manufactured around 1925.
Courtesy of Rick and Pamela Stevens. $300

The graphic image of an Indian chief in war bonnet spiced
up this Calumet Coal sign considerably. Although it has
endured some hard times, the graphics will help keep
this historical piece in the limelight. It measures 18" x
22" and dates to the 1930s.
Courtesy of John Bobroff. $400

Railroad advertising has always been highly collectable.
This Santa Fe porcelain sign measures 10" x 10" and is
in beautiful original condition. It dates from the 1930s.
Courtesy of Bob Mewes. $1,500

Scranton, Pennsylvania,
was home to Interna-
tional Salt Company.
The large graphic of
its retail package along
with a prominent five-
cent price gives plenty
of sales impact. In ad-
dition, their pouring
saltshaker tops it all
off for eye appeal. This
piece dates from the
1920s and measures 11"
x 22".
*Courtesy of Bob New-
man. $1,250*

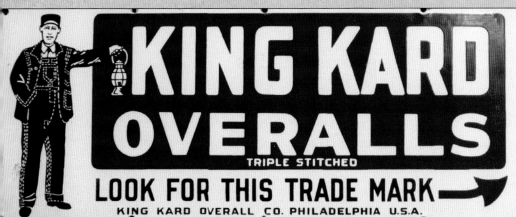

Outstanding condition combined with wonderful graphics make this King Kard Overalls sign extremely desirable. Overalls were worn in many of the trades, but railroad worker themes seem to be prevalent on most of Overalls advertisements. This one measures 10" x 31" and dates to around 1915.
Courtesy of Bob Newman. $3,000

Here's an eye catcher! The serviceman's dress makes this graphic Petro Oil Burner sign easy to date to the 1920s. Oil heat was beginning to be quite popular as an alternative to coal by this time. The sign was manufactured by Baltimore Enamel & Novelty Company of New York and measures 30" x 21".
Author's collection. $1,800

This 24" round M & M Ice Vending Co. sign depicts a tuxedo-dressed penguin carrying a leaking bag of ice. All advertisers try to feature graphics that will catch the public's imagination. This one got the job done.
Private collection. $400

Certainly one of the more spectacular of the die-cut milk bottle shaped dairy signs is presented here on this advertisement from W. H. Blackmer of Athol, Massachusetts. It measures 24" x 10" and dates to around 1930. *Courtesy of Bob Newman.* $2,200

"WE MAKE OUR OWN ICE CREAM"

MILK FOR HEALTH

W. H. BLACKMER

ATHOL, MASS

The 1930s saw production of this Newport Ice sign with its classic snow-capped lettering, which was used by many of the ice producers. It measures 15" x 29". *Courtesy of Bob Newman. $550.*

This triangular-shaped Imperial Ice sign, measuring 23" per side, dates from the 1920s. *Private collection. $200*

A California favorite, Foster's Freeze had a variety of porcelain enamel signs produced for them over the years. The fantastic foursome shown here are smaller sized, as seen by the proportion of the grommet holes. They are all highly collectible and the ones shown here are in like-new condition. They date from the 1940s and measure, left to right, 12" x 6", 13" x 9", 7" x 8", 8.5" x 10". *Courtesy of Bob Newman. $450, $900, $450, $900*

I took a separate close up of the fifth and most valuable member of the set. Its eye-catching graphics make this ice cream cutie very desirable. It measures 10" x 7" and like the rest, dates from the 1950s. *Courtesy of Bob Newman. $1,500*

This large-sized Lawrence Barrett Cigar sign measures approximately 48" x 24". The beautiful central image was done with a decal fired onto the porcelain. It was manufactured by Bellaire Stamping Company as evidenced by the "B.S. Co. 52 State Street, Chicago, and Beaver Falls, PA" ink stamped at the bottom. It dates to around 1915.
Courtesy of Jeff Kaye. $1,100

An unknown manufacturer produced this beautiful die-cut menu board for Canham's Ice Cream, possibly in the 1930s. It measures 28" x 11" and comes with its original menu inserts.
Courtesy of Dick and Diane Kinsey. $1,800

Madison, Wisconsin, was home to the Mansfield-Caughey Co., which had this Pasteurized Ice Cream sign produced sometime around 1930. It measures 24" x 18". Intertwining letters such as the ones seen at the top of the sign was a popular way to create an advertising logo for dozens of early American companies.
Author's collection. $600

Another fine example of great looking graphics can be found on this cement company sign—this one being from Iron Clad Portland Cement of Glen Falls, New York. It measures 15" x 15" and dates to around 1915.
Courtesy of Dick Marrah. $800

The bigger the product appears on a sign, the better the message gets across. Case in point is the loaf of bread seen on this Master Big Loaf Bread sign dating from around 1950. It measures 25" x 44". *Courtesy of Jeff Kaye.* **$500**

Another porcelain sign with a familiar logo—American Airlines—dates from the 1950s. *Courtesy of Bob Newman.* **$400**

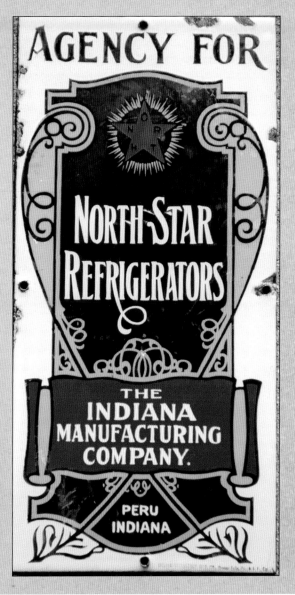

Here's a busy little piece. This North Star Refrigerators sign was manufactured by Ingram-Richardson. Many of the existing North Star signs have lots of acid etching and rust stains. This example is definitely the exception. Note that some of the early demonstration signs done by Ingram-Richardson are similar in appearance to the many fancy scrolls seen on the North Star sign. It measures 16" x 8" and dates to around 1920. *Author's collection.* **$900**

A commercial-sized refrigerator was probably the intended use for this 12" x 22" Dry-Kold porcelain sign from around 1940. *Courtesy of Rod Krupka.* $300

The world's motion picture headquarters is to this day located in Southern California. Although most of the larger studios were well equipped with backdrops, lighting, and other sundry production items, some things were best left to outside sources. Such is the case on this Ralph McCutcheon advertisement from the 1950s. Filming "westerns" was big business during this era and the McCutcheon enterprise could provide enough livestock saddled up and ready to go for the largest of productions. It measures 12" x 42". *Courtesy of Jeff Kaye.* $1,000

At first glance this 18" diameter advertisement appears to be something related to the automobile industry. However, a quick scroll to the bottom will show it's actually promoting cigar sales. It dates from the 1930s. *Courtesy of John Bobroff.* $650

Reproductions can be widely found in the advertising marketplace with porcelain signs being no exception. This graphic Texas Electric Service sign measures 36" round and has a gray porcelain back. Reproductions have been manufactured that look identical on the front, but can be easily identified by its having white porcelain on the backside.
Courtesy of Bob Newman. $1,200

A huge competitor in the ever-growing cigarette market was produced by the Lorillard Company under the trade name Murad. Their brightly colored package of cigarettes is seen on this 3.5" x 22" advertisement dating from the 1920s.
Author's collection. $750

A close-up shot of the Murad graphics reveals its fine attention to detail. This could only be achieved with the use of the fired-on decal process.
Author's collection.

This scarce Camels sign features an open pack of their popular brand. It dates to around 1950 and measures 4" x 26".
Courtesy of Bob Newman. $700

The Poultry Producers of Southern California utilized this Calawhite Eggs sign in the 1930s. It measures 9" x 20".
Private collection. $300

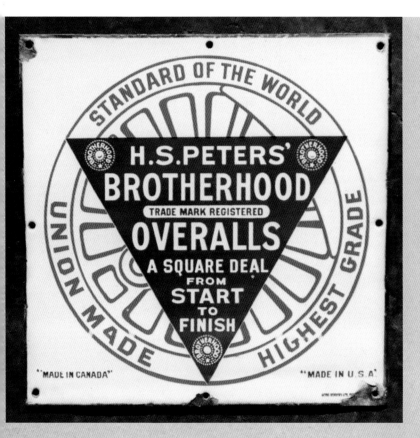

Acton Burrows of Toronto produced this H. S. Peters Brotherhood Overalls advertisement in the 1920s. Like most of the other Overalls advertisements of the era, it had a railroad theme, superimposing a triangle over a drive wheel of a steam locomotive.
Courtesy of John Bobroff. $400

Even to this day the railroads are the exclusive haulers of bulk coal. However, much has changed in the industry where in today's market it appears only power plants are the ones that take delivery. The large empty space at the bottom of the sign was meant for the local distributor to stencil with paint their company's name, city, and address. This was done primarily on tin signs and is seldom seen on porcelain advertisements. It measures 14" x 24" and dates from the 1920s.
Courtesy of John Bobroff. $500

The Pure Foods and Drug Act of 1906 prevented words such as "cure" being used on medicinal advertising. That makes this piece an early one, dating to prior years. It measures 6" x 16".
Courtesy of Mick Hoover. $800

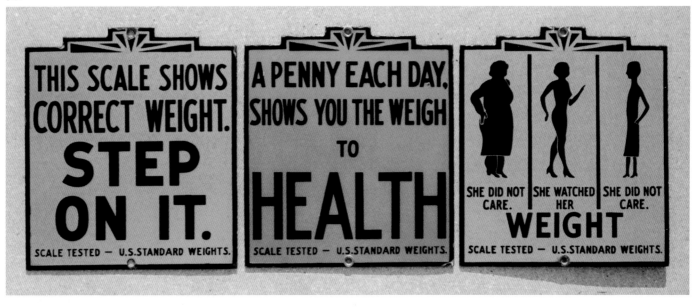

The porcelain trio shown here were used on public penny weighing scales. These scales were common in drugstores and sidewalks through the 1950s and offered the public a way to keep tabs on their weight. The sign on the right picturing the silhouettes of the three women is notably the most common. It has peculiar, if not humorous, graphics. The other two are much more scarce, but not quite as eye appealing. They all measure 10" x 9".
Courtesy of Mick Hoover. $300 each

Modern, but graphic, this Jorgensen Steel sign dates to the late 1950s. It measures approximately 14" x 14".
Courtesy of John Bobroff. $500

Socony Motor Oil decided the direct approach was the best approach on this 15" x 14" advertisement from the 1940s.
Courtesy of Mick Hoover. $400

This 10" x 14" New Process Laundry Co. sign dates to the 1930s.
Courtesy of Mick Hoover. $450

Baker Ice Machine Co. of Omaha, Nebraska, got the message across with this cute little oval sign to be placed on their equipment. I'm getting cold just looking at it. This one measures 5" x 12" and dates from the 1930s.
Courtesy of Rod Krupka.
$250

Check out the exceptional graphics on this die-cut Shepherd's Launderers porcelain sign. This advertisement dates to the 1930s, when Shepherd's had stores located in Beaumont and Houston, Texas. It measures 15" x 30". Note the black sheep in the center of the herd. Simply beautiful!
Courtesy of Bob Mewes.
$3,000

Reddy Kilowatt graced the advertising of most of the larger electric companies. However, many of the smaller rural companies let Willie Wiredhand take center stage—as is the case on this 18" round Farmers Electric Cooperative sign from New Mexico. It dates to the 1950s.
Courtesy of John Bobroff.
$450

Rare indeed is this unusual Headlight Shrunk Overalls sign. It is somewhat similar in appearance to the normal Headlight Overalls sign. However, a more than cursory glance will reveal the many differences between this rare piece and its similar cousin. Most notably it touts the anti-shrinking capabilities of their products. It measures 11" x 21" and dates to the 1930s.
Courtesy of Bob Newman. $1,500

This 18" round Sweet-Orr clothing sign features its well-known men having a tug of war logo. It dates from the 1920s.
Courtesy of Bob Mewes. $1,300

Here's an unusual piece. This eight-sided sign was used on a penny scale. If you look closely, it says "Manufactured by Watling Scale Co., Chicago." They were not the manufacturer of the sign, but the scale on which it was used. Watling was a very large company that manufactured many different items, most of which were all mechanical in nature, including slot machines, trade stimulators, and other amusement devices. The year 1933 is also marked on the sign.
Courtesy of Rod Krupka. $400

This 30" round Speedoleum Motor Oil sign dates from the 1920s.
Courtesy of Rod Krupka. $800

This large-sized 36" x 24" Hubbard's Superlative Flour sign dates from around 1915. The rope-bordered logo seen on its central image was probably used as the manufacturer's label on the end of their barrels.
Author's collection. $1,700

This Del-Monte Food Products sign measures 20" x 24" and dates to 1950.
Courtesy of Darryl Fritsche. $500

Always a favorite, Hires Root Beer is advertised on this 11" x 27" sign. The slogan, "The Spot to Stop," must have been short-lived as it is quite unusual.
Courtesy of Bob Newman. $700

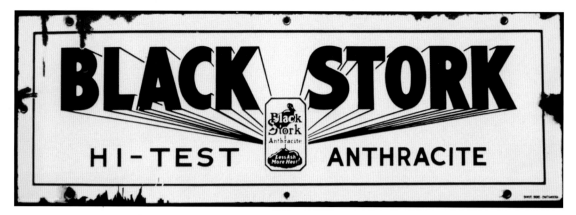

Here's an unusual piece. It's too bad the Black Stork logo seen in the center isn't larger, as it has lots of eye appeal. It measures 10" x 30" and dates to the 1930s.
Courtesy of John Bobroff. $300

One of the most unusual parts of this **Black Stork Anthracite** sign is its manufacturer. Here's a close-up of the ink stamping on the bottom right corner.
Courtesy of John Bobroff.

Caloric Furnaces advertised with this large lettered sign in the 1920s. It measures 13" x 36".
Courtesy of Long Beach Antique and Collectible Mall. $350

Castle Gate was a large manufacturer of coal located in Utah. This 12" x 30" advertisement was produced sometime around 1940.
Courtesy of Jeff Kaye. $400

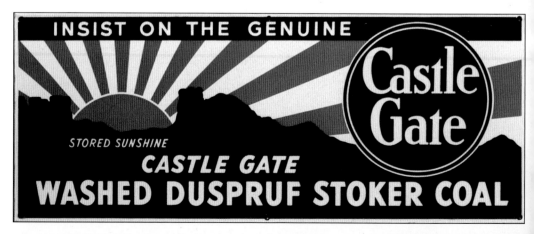

A beautiful example of a minuteman decal is seen on this Continental Fire Insurance Company sign dating to around 1915. Although no manufacturer has left ink stamping to designate its lineage, it's a fairly safe bet, due to the complexities involved in the graphics and firing process of the decal, that this piece was done by one of the larger manufacturers of the time. Measures 12" x 16".
Courtesy of Bob Newman. $1,400

Continental Fire Insurance Co. of New York used this graphic sign sometime around 1915. The central image of the minuteman was done with a decal that was fired into the porcelain. It measures 18" x 12".
Courtesy of Bob Newman. $2,000

The wonderful attention to detail seen on the Continental Insurance sign calls for a close-up of the graphics. The image of the minuteman was done in a separate process with a decal, which was fired onto the white base coat of the sign. It is too bad more of these decals were not applied on other porcelain signs as they make any sign a lot more eye catching.
Courtesy of Bob Newman.

The 1920s saw production of this White Star Laundry and Dye Works porcelain sign. It measures 14" x 20" and is ink stamped at the bottom right, "Baltimore Enamel & Novelty Co, MD." *Courtesy of John Bobroff.* $650

It appears this Indian Echo Cave die-cut sign was meant for mounting on a post. It is unlikely, though, that the Pennsylvania Highway Department had anything to do with it. It measures 32" x 24" and dates to the 1930s. *Courtesy of John Bobroff.* $600

Destined for use in a pharmacy, this *Los Angeles Times* sign dates to around 1920. It measures approximately 30" x 18". *Courtesy of Bob Newman.* $800

Here's a great sign from International Mercantile Marine Lines. Most likely this sign was placed near port areas, probably on the eastern seaboard, but it's hard to say for sure. Although it may appear that this piece has overseas origins, it actually was designed for use in North America, as well. J. P. Morgan funded this conglomerate of shipping companies, which involved many people in the United States and Canada. The five flags on the right side dress up this sign considerably. It dates from the 1920s and measures 15" x 17".
Courtesy of Mick Hoover. $1,200

Howell, Michigan, was home to this 9" x 20" agency sign in the 1920s.
Courtesy of Mick Hoover. $350

This beautiful large-sized California Reserve Co. sign dates to around 1920. It measures 44" x 32" and, as evidenced by the four holes near its top, was part of a neon display. Obviously, the bank was proud of its head office building, which was located in Los Angeles. Notice the detail work, the streetcar and automobile traffic near the bottom. A beauty!
Courtesy of Sue Gladden. $4,000

Sullivan Fence Construction Co. of Los Angeles, California, utilized this 6" x 12" sign in the 1950s. It has an interesting arrangement of holes, no doubt for placement on several styles of fencing.
Courtesy of Sue Gladden. $150

Sanders is a well-known name in Michigan. This small-sized 2" x 4" Chilly Boy sign might have been used on a cooler. *Courtesy of Mick Hoover.* $100

Porcelain had many uses other than advertising. Porcelain lined refrigerators was the theme on this Glacier Agency sign dating from the 1920s. It measures 14" x 16". *Courtesy of Mick Hoover.* $350

Veribrite Signs of Chicago, Illinois, produced this 60" x 15" Sinclair Opaline Motor Oil sign sometime around 1930. It's ink stamped with the maker's mark at the bottom right. *Courtesy of Mick Hoover.* $1,150

Another popular American soft drink was Orange Crush. "Made from fresh oranges" was their signature slogan for years. The highly graphic display of their product in front of fresh oranges gave the desired impact. If you look closely, you can see their trademark, which dated back to their earliest years within a triangle. This beautiful sign dates from sometime around 1930 and measures 10" x 30". *Courtesy of Bob Newman.* $1,400

The California Wool Growers Association produced this beautiful reward sign sometime around 1925. As rewards go, $150 was substantial considering the era. Of interest to note is that the reward was not only paid for someone stealing sheep, but also stock piled wool that may be laying around in storage. Not to be overlooked, the central image of a mother sheep with her two babies is just outstanding. It measures 12" x 19".
Courtesy of Jeff Kaye. $400

This 3" x 18" Star Soap strip sign could have possibly been used as a door push. It is early, dating prior to 1930.
Courtesy of Bob Newman. $600

It is difficult to say whether this Zerozone Refrigeration sign was meant for mounting in a residential apartment complex or on a commercial building. As noted previously, many apartment buildings contracted out refrigeration units in multiples, therefore getting an advertising sign to be placed on the property. Of course, commercial users were also able to acquire this sign. It measures 7" x 12" and dates to the 1930s.
Private Collection. $200

Several different types of signs have been manufactured showing apartment rooms being available. Shown here is one advertising Montgomery Ward and Company's Trukold Refrigeration systems. Landlords who purchased multiple Trukold units were entitled to one of these signs. Note the two small porcelain rectangles off to the right side. The sign, when new, actually came with four of these, which were used to cover up whatever number of apartments was not available. Measures 15" x 18".
Courtesy of Mick Hoover. $450

Another variation on apartment signs. Again seen with two of the covers for the numbers. Measuring 16" x 14", it's ink stamped "Nelke-Veribrite Signs New York" and dates to the 1930s.
Courtesy of Mick Hoover. $525

Some fraternal organizations and clubs actually had their own porcelain signs produced for them. The example shown here was from a driving club located out of San Diego, California. The words "Tierra Del Sol" means "land of the sun." The best part of their logo is the sketch of the sun hanging on for dear life to the black outline. This piece most likely dates to around 1950 and measures 9" in diameter.
Courtesy of Jeff Kaye. $450

Here's another example of a club having its own porcelain signs produced for them. Nice western graphics gets the point across. If you look closely, you can see the manufacturer's mark above the word "Riders." It says, "Cameo 56, Los Angeles," which of course indicates it dates from the 1950s. This one measures 9" in diameter.
Courtesy of Jeff Kaye. $450

Here's a nifty pair of motel signs that were produced for the American Motel Association. Although only one of the two signs is marked as such, it is obvious by the graphics that both signs were produced for the association, mostly likely by the same manufacturer. They both measure 18" x 24".
Courtesy of Mick Hoover. $600/pair

You'd be hard pressed to not see the sales impact of this graphic American Marine Paint Co. sign. Large product cans combined with multiple colors make an impression that is tough to ignore. This piece dates from around 1935 and measures 18" x 27".
Courtesy of Jeff Kaye. $1,500

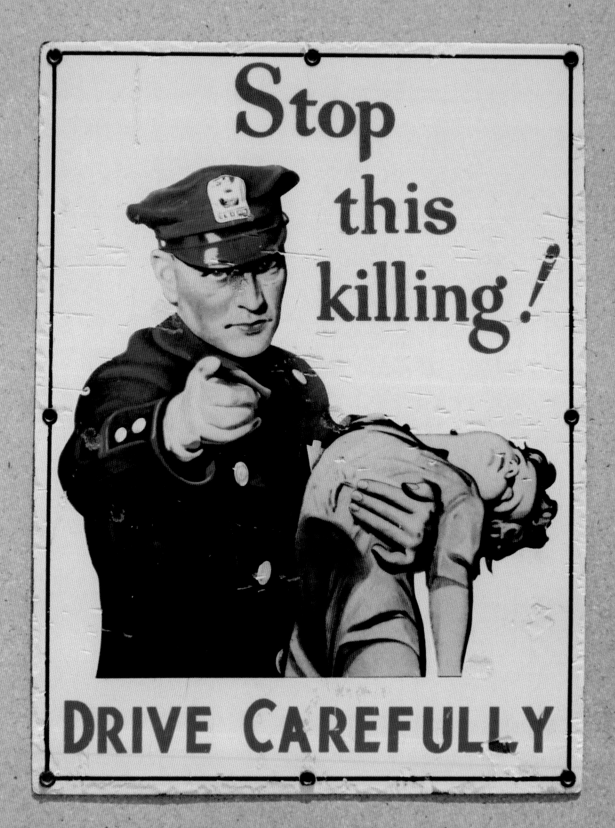

Stop this killing!

DRIVE CAREFULLY

Not the most pleasing image to be posted roadside, this 24" x 18" Drive Carefully sign conveys a powerful message. As unpleasant as its theme may be, the graphics on this piece are quite spectacular. It dates from around 1930.
Courtesy of Mick Hoover. $1,600

Many of the prominent American companies had subsidiaries in Canada. Although this Carhartts advertisement appears to be very much a part of the American scene, its actual use was in the Canadian marketplace. It features their wonderful railroad car superimposed on a red heart background at left. Measuring 8" x 35", it dates from the 1920s.
Courtesy of Bob Newman. $1,000

A close up of the manufacturer's stencil at the bottom right of the Carhartts sign.
Courtesy of Bob Newman.

Seven Oaks Dairy of Summerville, Massachusetts, used this large 30" round sign on the sides of delivery trucks. Most likely this dates from the 1930s. Although difficult to see at the bottom center, it's ink stamped "Baltimore Enamel & Novelty Co., Balto" and "17 Eustice Street, Boston."
Courtesy of John Bobroff. $1,200

Those of you who have ventured to Death Valley, California, will recognize at least a couple of the towns on this 25" diamond directional sign. The Auto Club of Southern California had these produced in the 1920s and 1930s to help motorists determine distances to towns and services. These directional signs were made for hundreds of locations and surface frequently on the Internet for sale. However, most are damaged considerably more than the one shown here.
Courtesy of Dick Marrah. $1,200

This little cutie measures a scant 4.5" square. It's exact use is unclear, possibly to be placed on trucks. One thing's for certain, it's fairly rare. It dates to around 1930. *Courtesy of John Bobroff.* $300

Even though they'd never make a guest spot on the show "Miami Ink," the chickens on this farm were given an indelible tattoo to prove ownership. To ward off potential thieves, this 11" x 15" sign was prominently placed on the farm. *Courtesy of John Bobroff.* $150

The infant pictured as the center image of this William A. McAdoo Milk sign stood out prominently, although somewhat ghostly. Unusual are the words "Tuberculin Tested" under the baby's image, as it brings to mind an American epidemic that was conquered by then. It dates to the 1930s and measures 16" in diameter. *Courtesy of John Bobroff.* $900

This unusual Children Only sign possibly found use on some type of amusement ride. Isn't it something that some people have to be told it's for kids only! It measures 5" x 16" and dates to the 1930s. *Courtesy of Mick Hoover.* $300

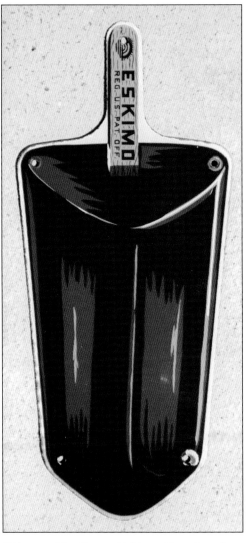

This Spicy Red Hots sign measures 4" x 11" and was used on one of its hot dog machines. It dates from the 1940s. *Courtesy of Rod Krupka.* $100

Bethlehem Steel used this simple advertisement in the 1950s. It measures 19" x 18". *Private collection.* $200

This graphic die-cut Eskimo Pie advertisement was meant for placement on the sides of trucks. It measures 16" x 7" and dates to the 1930s. Looks good enough to eat. *Courtesy of Dick and Diane Kinsey.* $1,250

Although no longer in business, Eastern Airlines left its mark on posterity with this 7" x 35" porcelain sign. The reverse side says, "Veribrite Signs, Chicago." It dates from the 1930s. *Courtesy of Rod Krupka.* $500

Shades of the deco era are showing on this Giampolini & Co. Painting sign. It measures 11" x 28" and most likely dates to around 1930. *Courtesy of Sue Gladden.* $450

Possibly designed for use on a local coal supplier's sales bin along with competing brands, this 3" x 9" Blue Coal sign is from the 1930s.
Courtesy of John Bobroff. $150

POSTAL MONEY ORDERS
ISSUED AT THIS OFFICE.

SAFETY AND SURETY OF PAYMENT GUARANTEED BY THE GOVERNMENT.

OBSERVE THE LOW RATES.

AN ORDER FOR $2.50 COSTS BUT 3 CENTS
$5.00 '' '' 5 ''

NO OTHER METHOD OF REMITTING SMALL SUMS OF MONEY IS SO SAFE OR SO CHEAP.

☞ ORDERS DRAWN ON 30,000 PLACES IN THE UNITED STATES.

CONFER WITH THE POSTMASTER IF YOU WISH TO REMIT MONEY TO ANY POINT IN THE UNITED STATES OR A FOREIGN COUNTRY.

The United States Postal Service had this Postal Money Orders sign manufactured in the late 1800s or very early 1900s. It touts the advantages of postal money orders, claiming their safety and the guarantee of payment that was offered by the government. Notice the small pointing hand at the bottom left. These pointing hands were a common part of the graphics on early porcelain advertising in the United States. This is a very early sign, as evidenced by the "Enamel Iron Company, Beaver Falls, Pennsylvania" ink stamp at the bottom center. It measures 9" x 7".
Courtesy of Pete Keim. $500

TELEPHONE PAY STATION KNOX TEL. & TEL. CO.

There were many small independent telephone companies throughout the United States. This early example is from the Knox Telephone & Telegraph Co. Dating to around 1910, it measures 2" x 25" and is ink stamped in the lower right corner "Baltimore Enamel & Novelty Co., New York."
Courtesy of Mick Hoover. $450

NATIONAL ASSOCIATION OF ICE INDUSTRIES · PLEDGED TO PURITY · FULL WEIGHT · GOOD SERVICE

Depend on **ICE** in all weather

Many times it is just not possible to pinpoint the exact use of a sign manufactured years ago. This National Association of Ice Industries sign is a case in point. It possibly could have been used on one of their coolers, but truck-side mounting or other applications are not out of the question either. It measures 14" x 14".
Courtesy of Mick Hoover. $400

The largest player in the competitive telegraph business was Western Union. Throughout the years they incorporated many designs and styles of signs. However, most of them featured few, if any, graphics—as is the case with this medium-sized 30" x 18" variety. Although Western Union is no longer in the telegraph business their yellow and black color scheme survives to this day as a symbol of their popular money wire transfers.
Courtesy of Mick Hoover. $350

This 20" round Goodrich sign dates from the 1920s.
Courtesy of John Bobroff. $725

Hastings, Minnesota, was home to this outstanding King Midas Flour sign dating from around 1920. Their familiar logo can be found on its porcelain thermometer as well. No, the girl is not scratching herself, but rather attempting to hold her dress in place as she stoops over a bit. Measures 36" x 24".
Author's collection. $2,300

Prudential Insurance Co. of America's famous rock of Gibraltar is pictured on this 5" x 30" strip sign. It's in beautiful condition for its age, dating to the 1920s.
Courtesy of Pete Keim. $425

70

This beautiful little **Safety First** sign was actually an advertisement for **Dragon Portland Cement**. It was common in the early part of the twentieth century to place Safety First signs around work areas. Most of the time the underlying advertisement was actually the dominant theme on these signs, which rendered the safety message all but useless. Such is the case on this 8" round example dating from the 1920s. I guess I'll have to bid higher next time — right, Mick?
Courtesy of Mick Hoover. $550

A more recent vintage is evident on this Oklahoma Tank Lines sign. It measures 17" in diameter and most likely dates from the 1950s.
Courtesy of Sue Gladden. $250

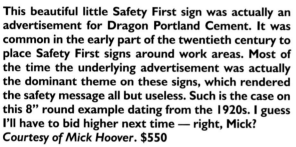

Five cents seems to be the universal price for early twentieth century cigars. The nickel list is long and Levenson Brothers was right there with the rest of them, producing its regional Boston-Smoker cigars. This five-cent cigar strip sign measures 3.5" x 21". Note the unusual abbreviation for the word "manufacturers." It dates from around 1915.
Courtesy of Bob Newman. $500

Many construction implements used porcelain signs to tag their manufacturer's image. Manning Maxwell & More, Inc. of Muskegon, Michigan, felt it was important to display their Load Lifter's 20-ton capacity. It measures 15" x 34" and dates from the 1940s.
Courtesy of Mick Hoover. $250

Guaranteed to scare the wits out of any employee, this stern warning was prominently posted in a Magnolia Petroleum Company bulk plant. Being one of the more gruesome warnings that I've seen on porcelain, it would certainly unnerve me enough to make sure I was paying close attention to the job at hand. It measures 9" x 14" and dates from the 1920s. *Courtesy of John Bobroff.* $200.

Possibly intended for use on a dispenser, this slightly tapered die-cut Betsy Ross Ice Cream sign measures 18" x 18" at its widest point. *Courtesy of Sue Gladden.* $250

A little rough around the edges, but nevertheless scarce, this Wrigley's sign has seen better days. Their slogan "After Every Meal" was used for years, but I have never seen another sign quite like it. It measures 14" x 36" and dates to around 1920. *Courtesy of Sue Gladden.* $425

Thick gloppy coatings were a giveaway to a sign's age on most of the early advertisements made of porcelain. It's quite evident on this sign and can be especially noticed around the word "Agency" at the top left. Combine that with the unusual lettering font and the five-cent cigar price tag, and you can just bet that this sign was manufactured sometime around 1910. It measures 10" x 15". *Courtesy of Pete Keim.* $400

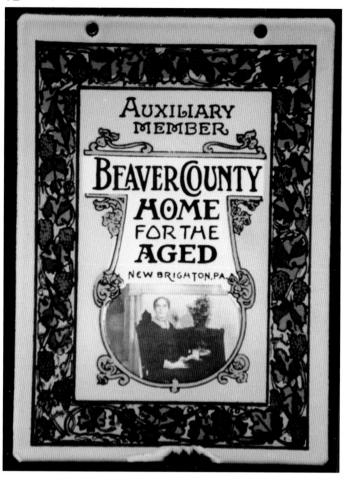

I'll give you one guess as to the most likely manufacturer of this beautiful little Beaver County Home for the Aged sign was. Any of us that have been doing this for a while should be able to pinpoint those familiar colors and graphics being from the early years of Ingram-Richardson. Combine this with Beaver County placed prominently on the sign, and all doubt is removed. It measures 8" x 6" and dates from around 1910. *Courtesy of John Bobroff.* $1,000

This small-sized 12" x 8" Just Suits Cut Plug advertisement is an ideal size for collectors. Considering it dates from around 1910, its condition is outstanding. *Courtesy of P. Keim.* $850

To ward off potential thieves, many commercial business owners utilized porcelain signs similar to the one pictured here. Most of these were regional in nature, being operated by the local alarm company. This one is from Central Watch Service, measures 6" x 9", and dates from the 1930s. *Courtesy of John Bobroff.* $250

Catchy graphics, especially those utilizing a price that was outdated at least seventy years ago, will make any sign an attractive addition to an advertising collection. This Goblin Orangeade sign is a case in point. It measures 18" x 13" and appears to date from the 1930s. *Courtesy of Sue Gladden.* $800

For years the name Dickinson's was known in the feed business. This poultry feed sign features its logo with a hen on a nest of eggs. It dates from the 1930s and measures 28" x 14". *Courtesy of Jeff Kaye.* $1,000

If you look closely at the central graphics of this King Coal sign, you can see the 'King' himself sitting on top of a large brick of coal. This sign measures 10" x 26" and dates from the 1930s. *Courtesy of John Bobroff.* $400

National Cigar was a well-known manufacturer with its own porcelain advertising signs. This one measures 3" x 36" and dates to around 1905. It's ink stamped at the bottom center "Balto Enamel & Novelty Company, Maryland" and "190 West Broadway, New York."
Courtesy of Pete Keim. $600

The 1940s saw this National Chinchilla Breeders of America sign manufactured. Note the unusual logo showing a chinchilla wearing a king's crown. I'm sure the SPCA had other thoughts. It measures 18" in diameter.
Courtesy of Sue Gladden. $650

For years Feen-a-mint Laxative Chewing Gum was a well-known and highly successful product. This 8" x 27" sign was manufactured in fairly large quantities and dates to the 1930s.
Courtesy of Mick Hoover. $650

Country store signs always look good in the kitchen. This Town Talk Bread sign is the ticket with its graphic baker and loaf of bread. It dates to the 1930s and measures 14" x 19".
Author's collection. $800

Graphics of the Sierra Nevada Mountains are seen on this 12" x 36" Sierra Ice Cream sign dating from the 1920s. Eilert Products Co. was the ice cream manufacturer located in Fresno, California.
Courtesy of Dick Marrah.
$600

Bloomington, California, was home to Pioneer Chain Link Fence Co. This 4" x 11" sign, like most all fence signs, was meant to be mounted directly to their product in a conspicuous location. It dates to around 1940.
Courtesy of Rod Krupka.
$75

There can always be some confusion about what type of enamel is being used on a sign. Many times the word "enameled" can refer to painted advertising. Although this 16" x 24" sign is obviously made of porcelain enamel, I'm only guessing that it is not advertising for porcelain enamel signs and window letters, as it appears to be referring to painted products. No matter which way it is, this is still an interesting addition to a sign collection.
Courtesy of Mick Hoover. $550

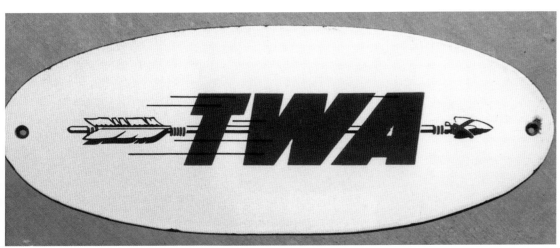

During the 1950s Trans World Airlines used a logo incorporating their initials superimposed over an arrow. Like most airline signs of this era, this example was primarily designed for use on the sides of trucks. It measures 7" x 17".
Courtesy of Jeff Kaye.
$400

Arden Dairy Products continued to be a huge western American advertiser for years. Their catchy logo of a fully suited child complete with adult-sized hat made for a high impact advertisement. This 36" x 21" oval sign is somewhat different than many of the other Arden porcelain signs. The most notable difference is the deep maroon color. Also a close examination of the child's face shows much more detailed graphics. Finally, Arden was sure to maximize their products' exposure by not only featuring the quart of milk held in the left hand of their famous delivery boy, but also by detailing out the packages of eggs and other products being carried by his right hand. The sign appears to date to sometime around 1940.
Courtesy of Jeff Kaye. $1,500

YOU ARE BIDDING ON THIS FOUR COLOR PORCELAIN ADVERTISING SIGN:(BODY)"DAVID DUFF & SON COAL ORDER HERE"(FORSET GREEN) "COAL(RE IS BORDERED IN BLACK,WITH FOUR POINTING HANDS OF TIME,FROM THE CORNERS OF THE SIGN TO THE CENTRAL ADVERTISING PART OF THE SIGN PHOTO'S)...MADE OF A VERY HEAVY GAUGE STEEL WITH A FOUR COLOR PORCELAIN OVERLAY.THE SIGN IS 17" X 17" @ 5 1/2 LBS,WHICH IS EXTREM HEAVY FOR A SIGN OF THIS SIZE... THIS SIGN HAS SIGNIFICANT IMPORTAN THAT DAVID DUFF WAS IN EARLY 1900'S, A PART OF THE CORPORATE BOD CITY NEW BEDFORD, MASSACHUSETTS . WITH THE PURCHASE OF THIS SIG COMES THE PROVENANCE...DAVID DUFF SOLD COAL TO COLONEL GREEN SOUTH DARTMOUTH, MASSACHUSETTS FOR THE WHALER SHIP : CHARLES MORGAN . HIS BILLS OF LADEN FOR THE COAL SALES ARE IN THE MYSTIC MUSEUM INC.OF MYSTIC, CONNECTICUT IN COLLECTION 19. THIS IS JUST / SUMMARY OF DAVID DUFF'S IMPORTANCE IN HIS ERA. THE CONDITION OF SIGN IS AS CLOSE TO MINT AS YOU CAN GET, WITH THE EXCEPTION OF A N (PENCIL ERASER SIZE) IMPERFECTION ON THE LEFT SIDE MIDDLE,THIS IMPERFECTION IS A RUST STAIN AND NO A CHIP... ALL 8 BRASS GROMETS PLACE PERFECTLY (SEE PHOTO) BID WITH CONFIDENCE, THANK YOU AND

A round advertisement encased within a square sign is seen on this David Duff & Son Coal advertisement dating from the 1920s. The fleur-de-lis pattern in the corners gave it some extra spice. The accompanying photograph will bring to light some of its history. It measures 17" square and dates from the 1920s.
Courtesy of John Bobroff. $500

Fortunately this sign's lineage has been partially recorded in this auction company sticker still affixed to the backside of the David Duff & Son Coal sign. One could only wish that all of our signs would carry a similar label, but unfortunately many of the early advertisement histories have been lost.
Courtesy of John Bobroff.

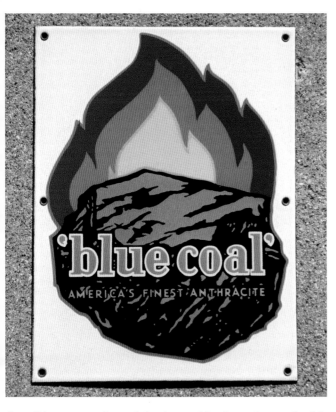

A well-known trademark in the coal business is seen in this 13" x 10" Blue Coal Anthracite sign. Although not obvious in the photograph, the porcelain on this sign is quite thick and has a high degree of shelving. It dates to around 1930. *Author's collection.* $450

Being a relatively obscure manufacturer, what this Brady's coal sign lacks in recognition is made up for in size. It's hard to miss the piece of coal pictured on this 21" round sign dating from the 1930s. *Courtesy of John Bobroff.* $450

Advertising graphics that feature an American Indian are always popular with collectors. A western motif was used in this Indian Tan Shoes product sign. As seen by the initials "S.F." at bottom right, Buckingham & Hecht, a company located in San Francisco, California, produced this product. It measures 12" x 18" and dates to around the 1930s. *Courtesy of Jeff Kaye.* $800

Not exactly the handsomest monkey I've ever seen, but Big Ben Davis thought enough of their furry fellow to prominently place him on their advertising. You want to be noticed? You got it with this one! It measures 23" square and most likely dates to around 1940. *Courtesy of Jeff Kaye.* $900

The 1930s was the heyday for neon advertising. There were literally hundreds of neon shops across America, all keeping busy with custom-designed neon signs. This small-sized 2.5" x 6" builder's tag was produced for Electrical Products Corporation. Hints of its deco-era lineage can be seen in its design.
Courtesy of Sue Gladden. $100

In the golden days of railroad travel, many depots offered Western Union wire services to the traveling public. This was also true of the nation's bus lines. To accommodate travelers, most of the intermediate or larger-sized bus and rail depots had waiting rooms and the Western Union sign displayed here was designated for such an area. It measures 16" x 33" and dates to the 1930s.
Courtesy of Mick Hoover. $450

Along with their popular automobile petroleum products, Sunoco also trademarked the name "Sunheat" for home heating oil. The black background offsets their red and yellow sun logo considerably. This eight-sided example measures 32" in diameter and dates from the 1930s.
Courtesy of Butch Greer. $800

One more competitor in the ever-growing market of automobile tires was a company called Acme. This Red Letter Tires sign dates to the 1920s and measures 12" x 30." It's ink stamped at the bottom right "Balto Enamel & Novelty Co, Baltimore and 200 Fifth Avenue, New York."
Courtesy of Mick Hoover. **$500**

Socony Petroleum utilized this 18" x 36" three-color sign to help promote their oil change service. It dates from the 1920s.
Courtesy of Mick Hoover. **$500**

Probably the most sought-after of all automobile-related porcelain signs is shown here. As if collectors would need any help dating this sign, the woman's dress should make it obvious that it dates from the 1920s. Although I have seen several of these Kelly Tires signs show up on the Internet and in my years of attending shows, they command the highest of prices due to the beautiful graphics and subject matter at hand. I wish they had made this sign in the tens of thousands, as every collector would like one. These signs were meant to be mounted as a pair and displayed back-to-back on top of a pole high above the ground. I actually know of a collector that has both of them intact and original. I am just happy to even be able to acquire one! It measures 42" in diameter.
Author's collection. **$20,000 plus**

As far as food product advertisements are concerned, you'd be hard pressed to find a more eye-catching design than this one produced for White Swan Brand. This multi-colored graphic beauty measures 30" square and dates from the 1920s. *Author's collection.* **$2,600**

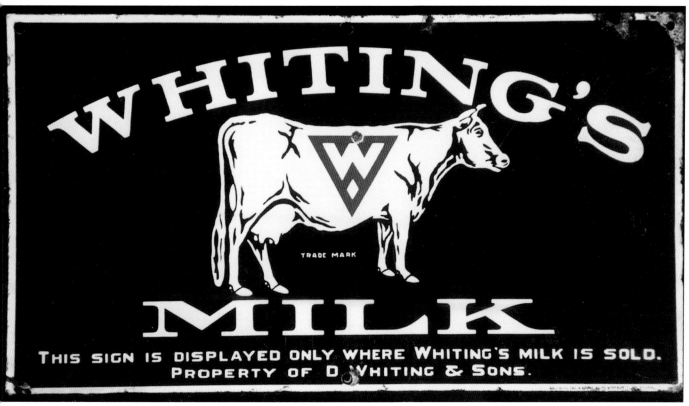

Whiting's Milk was manufactured in Boston, Massachusetts. Like many dairy producers, Whiting's found a cow to be a most natural choice for a trademark. It measures 11" x 20" and is ink stamped at the bottom, "Baltimore Enamel & Novelty Company, Balto" and "17 East 11th Street, Boston." It dates to the 1930s. *Courtesy of John Bobroff.* $700

A restaurant in Texas was home to this most unusual Chickburger Sanwich sign. Notice the misspelling of the word "sandwich," which no doubt was intentional. The exact placement of this sign is anybody's guess, but the thickness of the porcelain combined with the 15-cent price tag helps date its manufacture in the 1920s. It measures 23" x 18". *Courtesy of Jeff Kaye.* $1,000

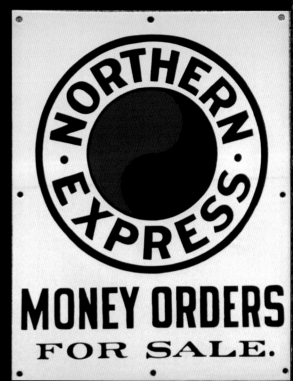

Designed for placement on the sides of Sinclair Petroleum stations, this Pennsylvania Motor Oil sign measures 60" x 15" and dates to the 1930s. It has a one-inch wide offset border going around its perimeter, which to collectors is known as being "self framed."
Courtesy of Mick Hoover.
$800

This unusual railroad crossing sign was a private production for the Chicago and North Western Line. It measures 24" x 18" and dates to around 1920. The ink stamping at the bottom right is an unusual one, being from Western Enameled Steel Sign Company, Chicago.
Courtesy of John Bobroff.
$800

Northern Pacific Railroad was not only a major passenger carrier, but was also in the express business. Additionally, they sold their own brand of money orders and utilized this three-color advertising sign to bolster sales. It measures 18" x 14" and dates from the 1920s. *Author's collection.* $850

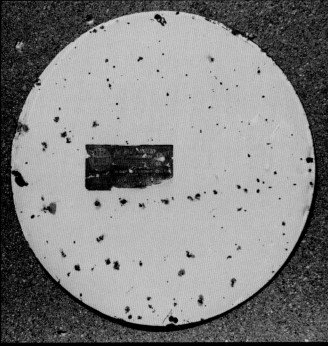

This beautiful Diamond Portland Cement Co. sign features a multi-faceted stone as its central logo. It measures 18" in diameter and dates to around 1920.
Author's collection. $650

Here's a shot of the reverse side of the **Diamond Portland Cement** sign. Having a paper label affixed to a sign for almost one hundred years is fortunate indeed. Many times even the most prominent manufacturers would not ink stamp their signs with a maker's mark, possibly at the advertiser's request. This left the factory to find other means to show who produced the sign by sometimes using a label. In any case, once their label became detached, the manufacturer has been lost to history. The label seen here is from **Ingram-Richardson**. *Author's collection*.

Seattle, Washington, was home to Pacific Fruit and Produce Co. One would only need to look at the graphic at the center of this 6" x 8" oval sign to date it from the 1920s. It was most likely used on the sides of delivery trucks. A beauty.
Courtesy of Jeff Kaye. $2,000

A local manufacturer of candy produced this 12" x 30" blue and white sign in the 1920s. Notice the pale blue outline on the perimeter of the lettering. *Courtesy of Long Beach Antique and Collectible Mall. $250*

What could have been a mundane advertisement was given partial salvation by the cartoon graphic of a policeman seen at the bottom left. At first glance it may be thought that Pendleton, Oregon, was the headquarters for National Corporation Services. However, a closer look would enlighten you to the fact that they were somewhere in the southern United States. It measures 8.5" x 10.5" and appears to date from the 1940s. *Courtesy of Jeff Kaye. $250*

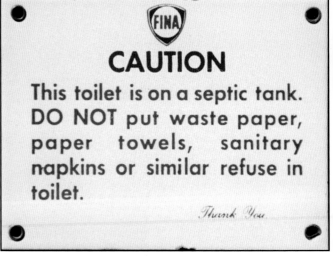

Small like a door push, but not used as one, would be this Hendlers Ice Cream sign. Most likely this was placed on a cooler or freezer that was part of the distribution process. They obviously made a number of these as evidenced by the prominent 4197 at the bottom center. Notice the similarity to the Sharpless Ice Cream sign seen earlier in this chapter—the same company obviously made both products. Measures approximately 5" x 7" and dates to around 1925. *Courtesy of Dick and Diane Kinsey. $500*

To ward off septic tank problems, Fina Petroleum used this small 4.5" x 6" caution sign in the 1940s. *Courtesy of John Bobroff. $300*

Although it's not known exactly which city utilized this stark warning sign, it's obvious they meant business. Many of the larger municipalities enacted their own sanitation laws in the early part of the twentieth century. Some of these regulations wound up being listed on similar porcelain signs, most notably the Spitting sign that was used in New York subways. It was learned that sidewalks could be a major contributor to unsanitary conditions; therefore most regulations involved sidewalk cleanliness. The word "Bowen" appears at the bottom left side of the sign and is possibly the jobber that handled dealings between the municipality and the manufacturer, as this company has not yet surfaced as a porcelain enamel manufacturer. Measures 10" x 12" and dates to around 1920. *Courtesy of Bob Newman.* $600

A most recognizable trademark even to this day is the famous Dutch boy with paintbrush in hand. This advertisement measures 34" x 26" and dates from the 1940s. It was most likely a section of a larger advertising marquee. It has a one-inch turned down flange running the entire perimeter of the sign. *Courtesy of Jeff Kaye.* $500

Even porcelain enamel manufacturers needed an effective way to help sell their products. Due to the nature of the domestic type signs being offered, it appears this porcelain advertising sign was trying to target mostly small businesses. Unfortunately, the actual manufacturer of this sign never left their name to trace its lineage. Judging by the graphics and the amount of detail work along with the coloration, it appears Ingram-Richardson would be a safe bet. It measures 22" x 16" and dates to around 1910. *Courtesy of Pete Keim.* $2000

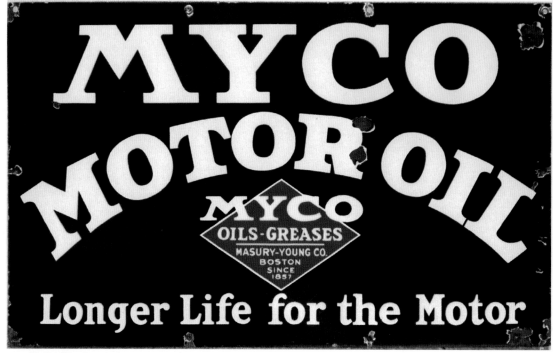

Boston, Massachusetts, was home to Masury-Young Co., producers of oils and greases. This Myco Motor Oil sign measures 16" x 26" and is most likely from around 1930. *Courtesy of Mick Hoover.* $600

Capital Airlines had this 12" round sign produced around the 1950s. *Courtesy of Bob Newman.* $400

Here is a newer advertisement for the famous Midwest soft drink, Vernor's Ginger Ale. It measures approximately 10" x 30" and dates to around 1950. *Courtesy of Rod Krupka.* $500

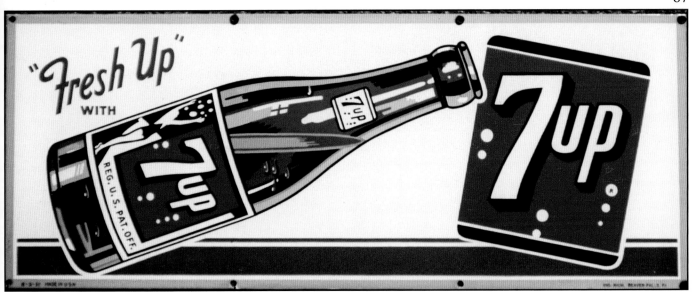

7up continues to be one of the largest sellers of soft drinks on the market. In the 1950s Ingram-Richardson produced this 12" x 30" graphic sign. It is embossed "Ing-Rich Beaver Falls PA" on the bottom right. The condition seen here is absolutely a standout. *Courtesy of Bob Newman.* $900

No questions asked about the location or the usage of this 15" x 18" sign from the Redlands Sanitary Laundry. The ink stamping at bottom right places it to being manufactured by California Metal Enameling Company. It dates from the 1920s. *Courtesy of John Bobroff.* $300

Although simply done in black and white porcelain, the eye-catching graphics on this Dexter Portland Cement sign greatly enhances its collectability. It measures 15" x 10" and dates from the 1930s. *Courtesy of John Bobroff.* $500

Stove and range producers spent millions of dollars advertising with high-quality graphic porcelain signs. Excelsior Stove & Manufacturing Company was one of the larger suppliers and their National Stoves & Ranges brand was a well-known trademark. This 24" x 18" three-color graphic sign featuring a red, white, and blue shield, American flag, and eagle is a standout and begs to command attention. Although it has seen better days, fortunately the lineage on this sign can still be traced to Bellaire Stamping Company of 52 State Street, Chicago. It dates from around 1910.
Courtesy of John Bobroff. $700

I would like to think that this American Neon Displays die-cut shield sign was designed for use on a huge neon sign. Its rather large 20" x 20" dimensions would appear to be too big for such a designation, but considering the fact that some neon porcelain signs are 25' across, maybe this isn't so farfetched. It dates from the 1930s.
Courtesy of Jeff Kaye. $350

Die-cut shields seem to be a popular shape for advertisers. Most notably Union Pacific Railroad, who uses a very similar design for their advertising even to this day. The Idaho State Highway Department took a liking to this idea as well, and adopted its graphics on this U.S. Highway 191 sign. Supposedly it was removed from service from an overpass bridge. It's ink stamped at the bottom center "Veribrite Sign Company, Chicago."
Courtesy of Mick Hoover. $1,800

How to Save Life from DROWNING

When a drowned person is brought ashore, don't wait for anything. If possible, send for a physician. But get to work, with your own hands.

Figure 1   *Hands on*

LAY the patient on his stomach. Extend one arm directly over head. Bend the other arm at elbow, and rest patient's cheek on hand, to keep the nose and mouth off the ground and free for breathing. Kneel, facing forward, and straddling patient's legs at the knees. Place palms of hands on each side of back, just above belt line, with your thumb alongside the fingers, the middle finger just touching the lowest rib, and the tips of fingers just out of sight. (*Figure 1*.)

Figure 2   *Pressure*

WITH arms held straight shift your weight gradually forward, causing pressure forward and downward on patient's back and counting slowly: one, two, three. (*Figure 2*.)

Figure 3   *Figure 4*
Release   *Rest*

SNAP your hands sideways, off patient's back. Swing your body back and relax, counting slowly: four, five. (*Figure 3 and Figure 4*.) Straighten arms, and repeat pressure.

Four movements: straight arm pressure, quick release, swing back, rest.
Repeat these regularly at about five second intervals, twelve times a minute.
If you don't hear air drawn in when you snap off your hands, feel in the patient's mouth for obstructions—such as a wad of tobacco.
And unless a physician takes charge, keep up work steadily till breathing begins, and continues naturally.
Then remove patient, on a stretcher and well covered, to a hospital or his home.

Don't get discouraged. Stick to it, for 3 or 4 hours if necessary.

This is the so-called Prone Pressure Method of Resuscitation. It is used also in cases of gas poisoning (including poisoning from inhaling automobile gas fumes) and electric shock.

THE HUMANE SOCIETY
of the Commonwealth of Massachusetts

Although this sign is not actually an advertisement, it gives an idea of the varied forms of signage produced in the porcelain enamel business. The Humane Society of Massachusetts had this beneficial "How to Save Life from Drowning" sign distributed for use at beaches and pools. It measures 18" x 11" and dates to the 1920s.
Courtesy of Jeff Kaye. $500

Several of the prominent 1950s airlines had porcelain signs manufactured for them to be used wherever needed. Most people believe they found their home on the sides of trucks. This one measures 12" in diameter.
Courtesy of Bob Newman. $450

BEAVER LUMBER

The 1950s saw this two-color 14" x 12" Beaver Lumber sign in use. If the intent was to produce a logo that would stick in the mind of the consumer, then they got the job done.
Courtesy of Rod Krupka.
$300

Lots of eye-catching graphics are in the corners of this 17" x 17" Pave-ol sign. It must have been a good product, as its usage seemed to be all encompassing. I gave up counting colors after ten. Seeing it was manufactured using a stencil, you just know this sign was fired repeatedly at the factory, making it a costly affair. It dates from around 1930.
Courtesy of Bob Newman. $850

South Gate, California, was home to Ruchti Bros. Baby Beef. This large-sized 26" x 34" graphic sign dates from around 1950. *Courtesy of Jeff Kaye.* $700

An attractive woman in uniform is presented on this American Institute of Laundering 15" diameter sign. Her hairstyle helps date this piece to 1925-1930. *Courtesy of John Bobroff.* $600

Reddy Kilowatt has been a favorite advertising figure for years. His image is seen on this 36" Pacific Power & Light Company sign dating from around 1950. *Courtesy of Jeff Kaye.* $1,200

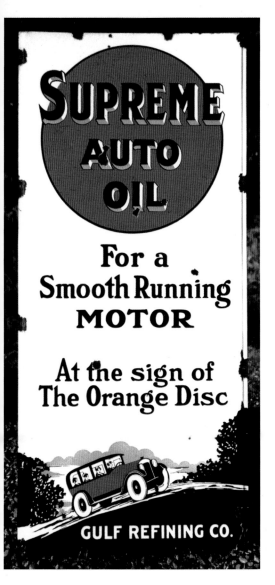

This eye-catching large vertical sign was produced for Gulf Refining Co. in the 1920s. Even though their famous orange dot logo with the words "Supreme Auto Oil" was the intended focus of this sign, most likely the touring sedan with occupants gets most of the attention from today's collectors. Along with a similar sign that has the word "Gulf" in the orange circle, this is the most graphic porcelain sign to ever be used by Gulf Refining Co. It measures 60" x 15" and was designed to be encased in a metal framework, which is evidenced by the half-inch offset around its perimeter. *Courtesy of Mick Hoover.* $1,600

Graphics such as those on this Supreme Auto Oil sign deserve a closer look. This is the kind of stuff that collectors clamor for! *Courtesy of Mick Hoover.*

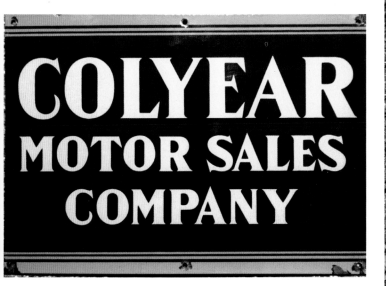

Colyear Motor Sales Company was a local automobile agency. This late 1920s advertisement measures 14" x 20". *Courtesy of Bob Newman.* $1,400

The unusual product manufactured for the J. E. Bauer Company on this die-cut paint sign seems to date from the 1940s. It measures 24" x 12". *Courtesy of Bob Newman.* $400

A popular coffee produced in the Pacific Northwest was the brand Ben-Hur. This 19" x 21" die-cut coffee can makes for an eye-catching advertisement. It dates from the 1930s.
Courtesy of Dick Marrah. $1,800

One of the most prolific advertisers in the feeds business was Park & Pollard Co. Their well-known trade name, "Lay or Bust," was used for many years. This advertisement dates from the 1920s and measures 7" x 20".
Courtesy of Jeff Kaye. $600

Ginger Ale with a golf theme seems to be the ticket on this 1930s Country Club advertisement. It measures 12" x 36". *Author's collection.* $450

A somewhat larger-sized advertisement from Monarch Cement was produced in the 1930s. It's another example of a manufacturer thinking up something like the great image at left that will wind up with today's collectors! It measures 15" x 40". *Courtesy of Dick Marrah.* $550

Many of the early beer manufacturers had signs produced for them with beautiful graphics. This 18" round Indianapolis Beer sign is no exception. A close inspection will reveal the "risqué" graphics of the woman, which some considered offensive at the time. It dates to around 1910. *Author's Collection.* $2,300

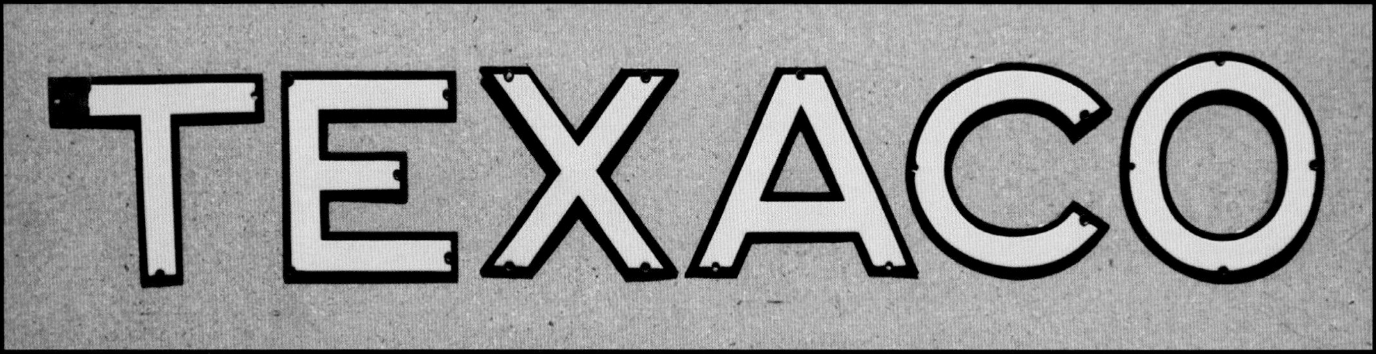

TEXACO

Service stations were notorious for using porcelain letters to advertise its company name or products. This allowed for a huge area to be covered that could be seen from a considerable distance. The thick individual porcelain letters shown here measure approximately 6" x 5" each. They've been placed closely together to be included in this combined photo. However, when in actual use they were separated from each other to give maximum advertising exposure. They date from the 1920s through the 1950s.
Courtesy of Mick Hoover. $600

Although several uses are possible, I believe this interesting ice cream bar sign was most likely used on those familiar bell-jingling, slow-moving mobile ice cream stores that go up and down city and neighborhood streets. Judging from the application of porcelain from the manufacturing process and the pricing used on the sign, this piece probably dates from the 1940s. It measures 20" x 10".
Courtesy of Sue Gladden. $800

ICE CREAM BARS

STRAW. COCONUT PECAN CRUNCH CHOCOLATE VANILLA MINT .20

SANDWICH VANILLA NEOPOLITAN .20 — POPSICLE .12
DRUMSTICKS .20 — FUDGESICLE .12
SIDEWALK SUNDAE .20 — BIG STICK .12
BANANA STICK .20 — ORANGE JUICE BAR .12
SNO CONES .20 — PUSH UPS .15
ESKIMO PIE .20 — 50/50 .12
ICE CREAM CUPS .20 SUNDAE CUPS .25 — KID BAR .12
CARNATION MALTS .30 — SPARKLE BAR STRAWBERRY SHORTCAKE CHOCOLATE ECLAIR .2

Here's something unusual. This 12" x 36" advertisement shows the Harbor Ship Supply Co. not only could provide maintenance equipment such as engines and deck supplies, but they also could stock the galley of your ship with groceries. What a combination! It dates from the 1940s.
Courtesy of Jeff Kaye. $650

Obviously designed for placement on the side of a delivery truck, this Borrego Freight Lines advertisement measures 16" x 24" and dates to around the 1940s.
Courtesy of Dick Marrah. $350

Several major newspapers across America used signs similar to this *Detroit News Daily and Sunday* one. Most likely it wound up in drugstores and sundry shops in the metropolitan Detroit area. It measures 7" x 18" and dates from the 1930s.
Courtesy of Mick Hoover. $350

Patten-Blinn Lumber Co. utilized this die-cut shield advertisement in the 1930s. They were located in Pasadena, California. It measures 17" x 15". *Courtesy of Sue Gladden.* $300

Eastern Air Lines utilized this eye-catching multi-colored advertisement around 1940. It measures 14" in diameter. *Courtesy of Bob Newman.* $600

The attractive graphics of the tobacco package has brought this Red Man advertisement to life. Again we see the image of the highly collectible American Indian on the Red Man package. It appears the sign dates from the late 1920s and measures 10.5" x 22". *Courtesy of Jeff Kaye.* $900

Considering the size of the apparatus that was to display this Northern Hi-Lift sign, its 4" x 7" dimensions would make it hardly noticeable. It dates from the 1930s. *Courtesy of Mick Hoover.* $100

The well-known Pennsylvania 100% Pure Oil trademark was utilized on this Pentex Motor Oil sign dating from the 1930s. Exclaiming a long service life of 1,000 miles seems paltry by today's standards. It measures 10" x 28". *Courtesy of John Bobroff.* $550

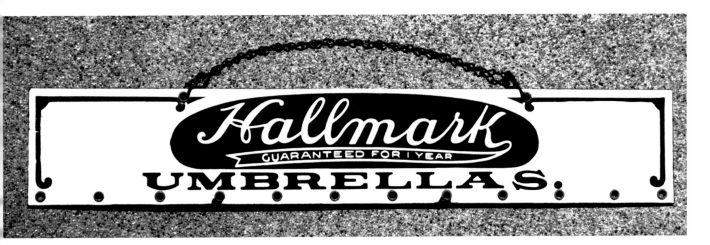

This Hallmark Umbrellas advertisement apparently doubled as an umbrella display holder in the 1920s. It measures 3" x 20". *Courtesy of Sue Gladden.* $300

Mason City, Iowa, was home to Northwestern States Portland Cement. This three-color advertisement dates from the 1930s and measures 15" x 18". *Courtesy of John Bobroff.* $350

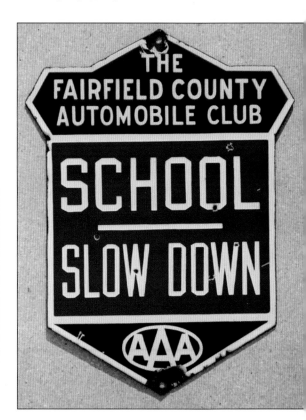

Another of the Western United States motoring enthusiast clubs was the Hemet Jeep Club. Their whimsical logo showing a trail-blazing goat smoking a cigar was sure to grab attention. This 9" round advertisement dates to the 1950s and has a rather strange mounting hole configuration.
Courtesy of Jeff Kaye. $450

A tough day at the shop was in store for the tool and die man that had to prepare the cut for this Producers Ice Cream sign. It probably wasn't much easier for those in the stenciling department either, as every color needed to be registered with no room for error. The end result was a most unusual and beautiful advertisement. I believe it dates to around 1930. It measures 20" x 9".
Courtesy of Jeff Kaye. $800

The Fairfield County Automobile Club had this die-cut shield sign produced in the 1930s. It was designed to be posted when vehicles were approaching a school. It measures 17" x 13".
Courtesy of Mick Hoover. $400

The *Detroit Free Press* is to this day one of the largest newspapers published in the Midwest. This 1930s advertisement would most likely be mounted on a pharmacy or sundries store. *Courtesy of Mick Hoover.* $350

Most likely earmarked for use on the sides of trucks, this die-cut Post Transportation Co. sign measures 12" x 20" and dates to the 1930s. *Courtesy of Sue Gladden.* $350

The like-new appearance of this IBP Laxative sign indicates that it was most likely in storage instead of in the public eye. This piece is quite unusual insofar as its busy wordings and graphics put space at a premium. The 1906 Pure Foods and Drug Act prohibited the sale of medicinal treatments that used the word "cure." Even though no promises were made on this 12" x 26" advertisement, they seem to be pushing the threshold when they are talking about their product being a remedy for as many ailments that are listed. I believe this piece to date from the 1920s. It is ink stamped on the bottom right, "Nelke Veribrite Signs, NY." *Courtesy of Jeff Kaye.* $1,250

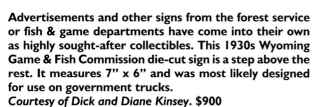

Advertisements and other signs from the forest service or fish & game departments have come into their own as highly sought-after collectibles. This 1930s Wyoming Game & Fish Commission die-cut sign is a step above the rest. It measures 7" x 6" and was most likely designed for use on government trucks.
Courtesy of Dick and Diane Kinsey. $900

Railway Express got into the air transportation business for several years in the 1920s and 1930s. This larger-sized Air Express sign features their winged logo and measures 36" x 36".
Courtesy of Bob Newman. $725

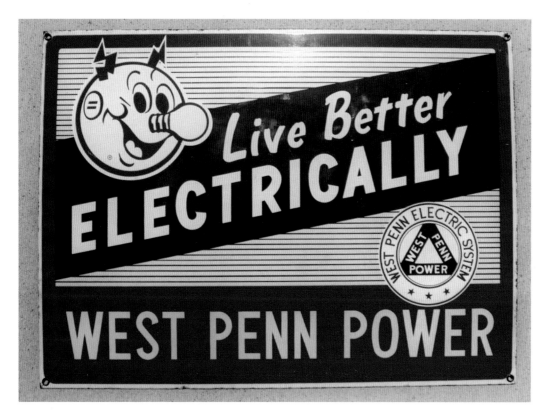

The image of Reddy Kilowatt is again seen on this Live Better Electrically sign from the 1950s. It measures 21" x 30".
Courtesy of Rick and Pamela Stevens. $900

SPARKLETTS

You've guessed wrong if you believe this 6" x 36" curved-bottom Sparkletts sign had anything to do with fireworks. The sparks coming from the top of each letter were there only to help identify the Sparkletts trade name that was used by a bottled water producer in Los Angeles, California. It is an early one, most likely dating prior to 1920.
Courtesy of Sue Gladden. $400

The National Recovery Administration was created by congress to help restore the country's economic well being in the 1930s—this 9" x 5" sign was proudly displayed by an independent member.
Courtesy of Rick and Pamela Stevens. $500

As indicated by the "10-6-53" ink stamp at the bottom right, this die-cut Texaco Distributor sign dates from 1953. It was common practice for bulk oil distributors to have their own porcelain sign featuring its name with the parent company's logo. This one is from Munising Coal Company, a local distributor in Michigan's Upper Peninsula. It measures 13" x 11".
Courtesy of John Bobroff. $450

Chapter Two:
Flat Two-Sided Signs

This chapter contains signs that were manufactured with advertising on both sides. Most of these were to be placed in a stand or frame of some type. This supporting method could be as small as a "lollipop" stand for sidewalk use, or as large as a filling station's main highway sign. Another method used frequently employed an iron bracket. Most of these brackets were simple in construction. However, some are so ornate that you wonder if they took first price in a blacksmith's contest!

The unusual logo found on this Crescent Ice Cream sign can be found in a die-cut form in the previous chapter. This one was a little bit less of a nightmare to manufacture, being of a simple rectangular pattern. It measures 20" x 30" and dates to sometime around the 1930s.
Courtesy of Dick Marrah. **$600**

Signs relating to bus companies have become highly sought after in recent years. Greyhound Lines was one of the more prolific advertisers in the bus transportation business. This beautiful die-cut advertisement is from a Greyhound Lines subsidiary in the west. Like some of the other Greyhound signs, a passenger bus is prominently figured. And, as always, their ever-present running greyhound makes the usual high impact visual image. To top it all off, this sign is two-sided. It appears that the puppy dog has injured its left front leg. A similar fate was avoided on its tail by the manufacturer placing porcelain that connected its tail halfway down its rear leg. It measures 24" x 36" and, as can be guessed by the graphics of the bus, dates from the late 1920s.
Courtesy of Dick Marrah. **$10,000**

Here's something you just don't see every day. This fantastic Santa Fe Trailways Bus Depot die-cut sign is truly a beauty to behold. Sporting its original iron bracket, one can see the unusual need for five hooks to suspend the sign. Most other manufacturers would have happily settled for two. A close examination of the bus reveals its marquee to read, "Chicago-Los Angeles." Still yet, its license plate tag gives away its birth year as being 1938. For collectors who are looking for something to wind them up, this should do it. Measures 23" x 25".
Courtesy of Dick Marrah. **$8,750**

A frame was designed to support this 30" x 24" Mona Motor Oil sign. Its die-cut pointed shape seems to complement the font style of the lettering, most notably all of the "O's" in the logo. It dates from the 1930s. *Courtesy of Mick Hoover.* $1,200

Not to be fooled by imitations, Waverly Motor Oil felt it was important to let the motoring public know they were purchasing products from one of their licensed dealers. This die-cut version measures 20" x 22" and dates from the 1920s. *Courtesy of John Collins.* $800

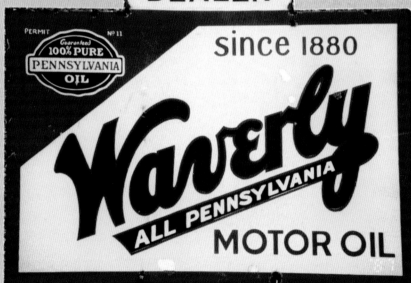

Burdick Sign Company had this Magnolene Motor Oils and Greases sign produced in the late 1920s. It measures 14" x 30". The ink stamping at bottom right reads, "Burdick Consumers Building, Chicago." *Courtesy of Mick Hoover.* $800

Designed to be supported by a bracket, this 1930s Arden Ice Cream sign features their famous child delivery boy with oversize hat. It measures 32" x 26". *Courtesy of Jeff Kaye.* $1,000

Even in the 1970s, you would be hard pressed to locate any type of bottled water for sale with the exception of those being distilled. Therefore, this Everpure Safe Water sign is most unusual as it dates from the 1930s. Its four mounting holes would suggest a one-sided advertisement, but this piece is definitely two-sided. It measures 12" x 9". *Courtesy of Bob Newman.* $400

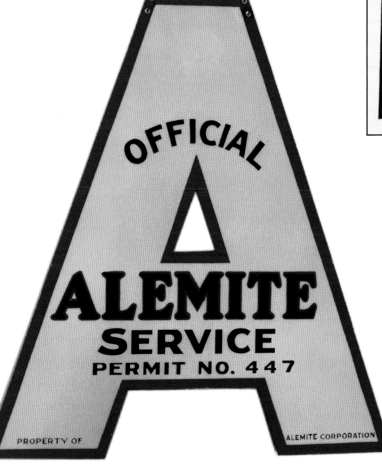

Alemite was a franchise vehicle service company. Their large 36" x 33" die-cut letter "A" was sure to instill a recognizable name to the motoring public. There will be no question as to who owned this sign as the fine print at the bottom notes, "Property of Alemite Corporation." *Courtesy of Mick Hoover.* $800

What appears to be a bucket is most likely a drinking cup filled with an ice-cold beverage. It was available on the menu at Mazzio's Pizza. It measures 18" x 16" and is somewhat newer, dating from the 1960s. *Courtesy of Darryl Fritsche.* $250

Veedol Motor Oils spent huge money on advertising through the years. This early die-cut sign dates from the 1930s and measures approximately 24" x 18". *Courtesy of John Collins.* $800

Even the 1940s saw signs with such outstanding graphics like on this 14" x 24" Interlux Paint sign. It was produced for International Paint Company, a huge manufacturer of marine paint. *Courtesy of Bob Newman.* $1,800

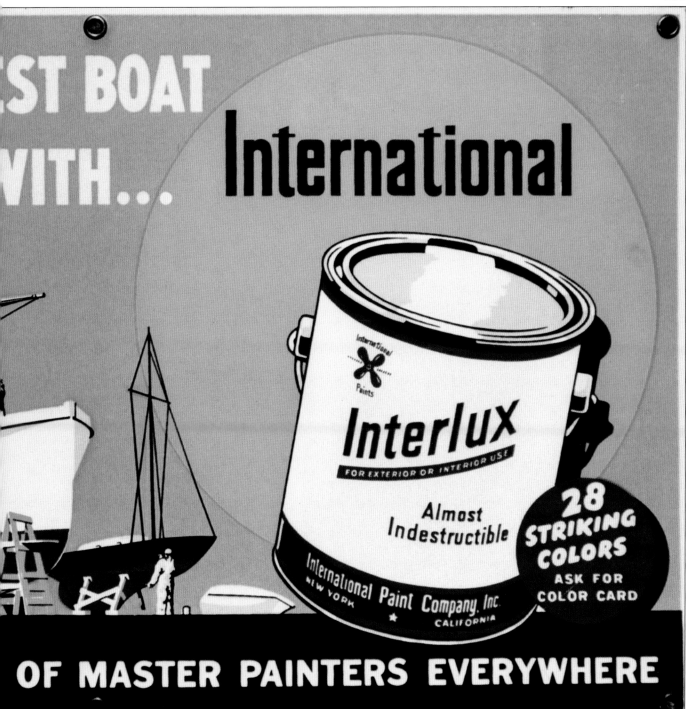

Here's an advertisement for a cola that was trying to compete with the many soft drinks of the era. Its small 2" x 6" size indicates its possible use on a dispenser, but there are plenty of other options as well. Of note is the font style that Celery-Cola incorporates. If it weren't for the blue and white color scheme, one would have to take a second look to realize that

this sign did not advertise a product manufactured by the world's foremost cola company, as indicated by the fancy tailings at the end of the script. This is an early piece, probably from around 1910. *Courtesy of Pete Keim.* $400

Although this 14" x 25" Goodyear Tires sign is similar in appearance to its flanged cousin, this two-sided version without flange is actually smaller and designed to be hung from a support bracket. It dates from the 1920s. *Courtesy of Bob Newman.*

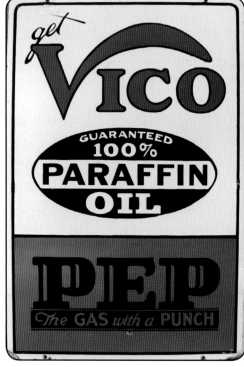

This 30" round Wilco Wheel Alignment sign was designed to have the graphics of a tire as seen by the tread pattern around its perimeter. Their aligning system involved the use of some type of cross-sight system, which is evidenced at the sign's center. It dates from the 1920s.
Courtesy of Gas Pump Ronnie. $750

Two separate products were advertised on this 36" x 24" four-color sign, which appears to date from the 1930s.
Courtesy of Mick Hoover. $900

As small as it is, this 4" x 11" Bluebird Records sign was meant to be viewed from two sides. It dates to the 1930s.
Courtesy of Mick Hoover. $200

Here's a piece that's "logo happy." The familiar Independent Oil logo can be spotted at the top left of this Northland Motor Oil sign, as well as the Pennsylvania Oil logo and Northland's own proprietary design. It measures 24" x 33" and dates from the 1920s.
Courtesy of Mick Hoover. $900

One of the many national brands of motor oil is advertised on this Sentinel Motor Oil sign. It is quite busy in nature, with the graphics of a soldier at guard and the two logos at center. I'm not exactly sure what type of dispenser they are referring to with their jargon of "non-refillable tanks." It measures 24" x 22" and dates to the 1930s.
Courtesy of Mick Hoover. $900

Designed to be hung from a support bracket, this Alemite Pennsylvania Motor Oil sign gives a clue to its 1930s deco lineage by its triple-layered keystone die-cut shape. It measures 30" x 22".
Courtesy of Mick Hoover. $950

Another major player in the motor oil business was the trade name "Havoline." Obviously, tampering by the local agency was a problem as they made it a point to let the consumer know that their product was distributed in sealed cans. It dates from the 1930s and measures 10" x 20".
Courtesy of Bob Mewes. $950

Still encased in its original steel frame, this 30" round Vico Motor Oil sign faithfully displays its message. These lollipop-style displays were utilized by almost all the larger petroleum manufacturers and were normally 30" in diameter. These could be conveniently placed where no other mounting apparatus was available. Even though these were popular in the 1920s and 1930s, many of these lollipop-style stands still survive to this day in collections. This one most likely dates from the 1930s.
Courtesy of Mick Hoover. $800

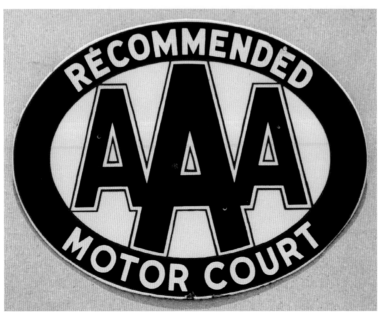

Through advertising attrition, it's rare to still find any porcelain advertising left intact in its original display location. With vandalism, change of design logos, company buyouts, collector liberation, and other miscellaneous motives, there just isn't much left still in service. Although this 18" x 24" oval AAA Motor Court sign is not seen on site, it is one of the few porcelain advertisements that was made in such quantity and has changed so little through the years that it can still be occasionally found giving faithful service at some motels. It was first used as a tourist guide starting in the 1930s.
Courtesy of Mick Hoover. $300

One of my favorite petroleum-related signs is this Harris Oils die-cut advertisement dating from the 1920s. Notice the clever usage of the barrel incorporated into their logo. It measures 14" x 17" and can also be found in a flanged version approximately the same size.
Author's collection. $2,300

America was the largest producer of automobiles in the world until relatively recently. Through the years there were literally hundreds of aftermarket manufacturers competing for automobile replacement parts business. One such company is advertised on this Duplate Safety Glass porcelain sign. Most likely dating from the 1930s, it measures 18" x 24".
Courtesy of Mick Hoover. $400

Although its 30" size might suggest this Red Crown Gasoline sign was used in a sidewalk lollipop stand, the placement of its many grommet holes around its perimeter indicates it would be able to function as a wall mount as well. It dates from around 1930. A similar sign with blue detailing in the center area can be found later in the book.
Courtesy of Mick Hoover. $1,000

One of the more rare petroleum-related advertising signs is seen here. This Olympic Refining Company advertisement has graphics showing a city superimposed on a mountain background. The bottom half shows an industrial area, although it does not appear that it has anything to do with a refinery. "Calpet" most likely is an abbreviated word for California Petroleum. Because Olympic Refining is the featured advertisement, it might stand to reason that some type of merger took place between a Washington State and a California-based refinery. Regardless, this is one rare bird! It measures 30" x 30" and dates from the 1920s.
Courtesy of Sue Gladden. $2,500

It's not unusual to see familiar manufacturers in other sideline applications—that's the case on this Goodyear Welt Shoe Repairing advertisement. For some reason or another, their well-known trademark did not appear on this sign. Possibly they reserved that for their automobile products only. It measures 18" square and dates to around 1930. The bottom right corner is ink stamped, "Property of Unit Repairing Machine."
Courtesy of Mick Hoover. $350

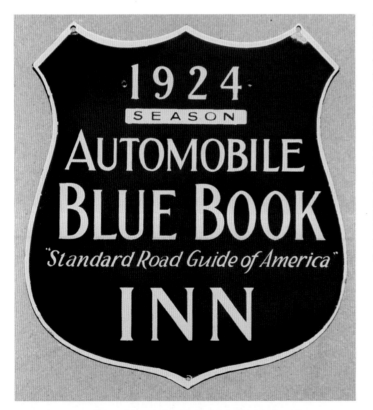

In the pioneering days of automobile travel, many motorists relied on the *Automobile Blue Book* to get them from one location to another. At this early stage in our highway development, establishments such as restaurants and lodging facilities were sometimes not easy to locate and gave the motorist a degree of trepidation when planning their trip. To help alleviate this anxiety there were several tourist guides published in these early years. These books would combine routing suggestions and maps along with much-valued information as to highway waypoints and features such as places to camp or stay. The Blue Book Inn advertisement seen here was given as a courtesy to the establishments that were registered and paid for inclusion in the *Automobile Blue Book*. Although this sign is dated 1924, closer examination reveals its intended use for future years as noted by the two grommet holes to each side of the date. Any subsequent years could be simply affixed to the sign. It measures 21" x 19".
Courtesy of Mick Hoover. $700

Meant to be displayed on a sidewalk lollipop stand, this Sinclair Pennsylvania Motor Oil sign features the outstanding dinosaur graphics that has become Sinclair's trademark through the years. It measures 24" in diameter and dates to the 1930s. *Courtesy of Greg Stevens. $1,700*

Long removed from its sidewalk lollipop stand, this 30" round advertisement for Polarine Oils and Greases still shares its legacy with collectors. It dates to around 1930. *Courtesy of Mick Hoover. $900*

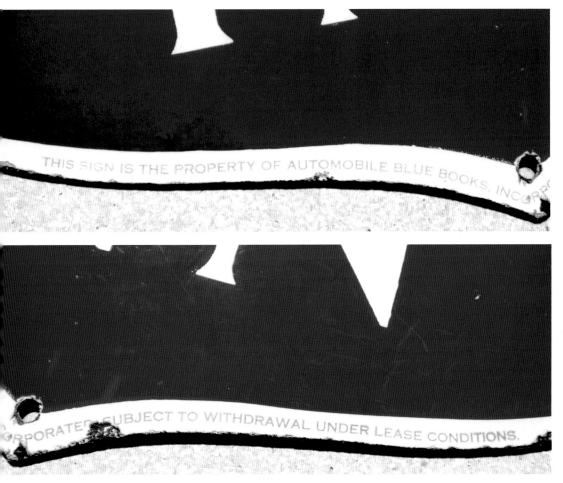

This has to be one of the longest porcelain enamel ink stampings on record. It deals with the proprietary information that the holder of the Blue Book Inn sign needed to know. Many porcelain signs advertised companies that were franchised in nature and would utilize a similar type of jargon ink stamped on their signs. Normally this can be found on the backside of one-sided signs, but the one shown in these two photographs has got to be a record breaker as far as its length. *Courtesy of Mick Hoover.*

Telegram delivery was big business up until the 1950s. This set of porcelain signs were designed for delivery bicycles. They each measure approximately 3" x 13" and date around 1930. *Courtesy of Mick Hoover.* $150 each

This three-color Goodyear Tires advertisement dates from the 1920s. It measures 12" x 24". *Courtesy of Mick Hoover.* $650

Ford Motor Company experimented with this die-cut logo in the 1920s. Along with its relatively short-lived design, Ford also came up with a slogan that was somewhat short-lived, calling its products "The Universal Car." This example measures 12" x 30". *Courtesy of Mick Hoover.* $1,800

Many of the oval **AAA** signs are common, but a closer look will reveal the uniqueness of the advertisement seen here. Not only is it rare because of its placement in the State of Idaho, but it also deals with a service station instead of a place of lodging. It measures 23" x 23" overall and dates from the 1930s.
Courtesy of Mick Hoover. $600

Manufactured as part of a larger unit, this die-cut pointing hand with the word "danger" appears to have the ability to be moved to different positions, as indicated by the large hole near its center. It measures 9.5" x 25" and is from the 1940s.
Courtesy of Sue Gladden. $550

Freedom, Pennsylvania, was home to Beaver-Penn Motor Oil. The bulldog emblem at the bottom left has fine print underneath that reads, "The Watch Dog of your Motor." It measures 18" x 22" and, as can be seen in the photo, is copyrighted in 1936.
Courtesy of Dennis Griffin. $2,800

Here's a variation on the Beaver-Penn Motor Oil theme. Somewhat similar in design and identical in measurement, I believe this advertisement to be somewhat newer than the previously shown example, if only by a few years. Notice the bulldog went for a walk.
Courtesy of Dennis Griffin. $2,500

This 21" x 18" National Automobile Club advertisement dates from the 1930s. Its exact use is uncertain, but many times automobile clubs promoted tourism, which might have placed this sign at a travel-related business such as a restaurant or hotel. It has a prominent spread eagle standing on a globe with the United States as its theme.
Courtesy of Mick Hoover. $650

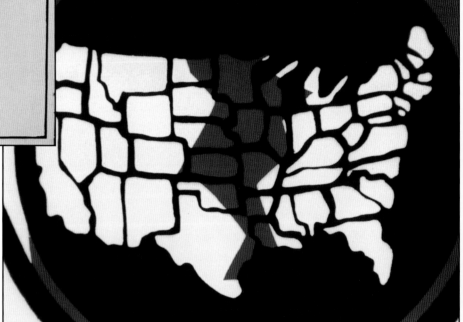

I thought you might like a closer look at the United States graphic near the bottom of the National Automobile Club sign. I must admit I've never seen the United States separated by such large divisions between the states. Also of interest is the zigzag red area, which might actually be a mistake on the part of the manufacturer.
Courtesy of Mick Hoover.

Polar bears have wound up being trademarks for a variety of American companies. This three-color Polar Bear Ice Cream sign dates to the late 1930s and measures 24" x 36".
Courtesy of Sue Gladden. $1,300

Tiolene was a trademark of the Pure Oil Company. This two-color 24" round advertisement dates from around 1930.
Courtesy of Bob Mewes. $1,150

Named after Detroit, Michigan, department store entrepreneur J. L. Hudson, the Hudson Automobile Company was founded in 1909. Ten years later the Essex trade name was first used by Hudson to introduce a new lower-priced line of automobiles that was designed to compete with models being produced by Ford and Chevrolet. This 16" x 30" advertisement is straightforward in design and to the point.
Courtesy of Mick Hoover. $1,100

This rare Midwestern beauty is one of only a couple known. For those of you not familiar with the word "Soo," it refers to the city of Sault Ste Marie, a town located at the eastern end of Michigan's Upper Peninsula. This 1920s advertisement measures 14" x 20", and at the bottom center, is ink stamped, "Burdick Enamel Sign Company, Chicago and Balto."
Author's collection. $3,000

Apparently fine whiskey is not the only thing that improves with age. Sinclair touted their Opaline Motor Oil to be mellowed for 80 million years as seen on this 30" round advertisement dating from the 1930s.
Courtesy of Bob Mewes. $1,700

Another in a long list of 30" diameter petroleum signs is this Vico Gasoline example. The "88" is an indication of the octane rating, which is on the high side considering this piece dates from the 1930s.
Courtesy of Mick Hoover. $1,500

Along with tires designed for use on automobiles, B. F. Goodrich was trying to target other markets as well. This Farm Tires die-cut sign was most likely intended for use at an implement dealership. It measures 11" x 24".
Courtesy of Bob Newman. $900

This beautiful Sunset Gasoline advertisement was most likely intended for use in a sidewalk lollipop stand. Its eye-catching graphics make quite an impression. A close examination will reveal a racing automobile at left and an early airplane at right. It dates from the 1920s.
Courtesy of Sue Gladden. $6,000

Always popular with collectors, the famous Hood Tires man is seen in a saluting pose on this 32" x 37" sign. What appears to be a red porcelain border is actually a metal frame, as evidenced by the two mounting tabs placed at the top. It dates from the 1920s.
Courtesy of Sue Gladden. $2,600

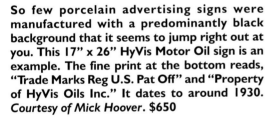

So few porcelain advertising signs were manufactured with a predominantly black background that it seems to jump right out at you. This 17" x 26" HyVis Motor Oil sign is an example. The fine print at the bottom reads, "Trade Marks Reg U.S. Pat Off" and "Property of HyVis Oils Inc." It dates to around 1930.
Courtesy of Mick Hoover. $650

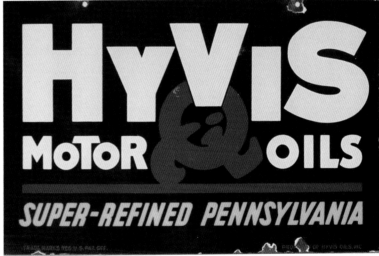

The late 1930s saw production of this Pacific Piston Rings sign. Dating a piece like this becomes no problem when its graphics show two cars racing around the image of an engine piston ring. It measures 15" x 23".
Courtesy of Bob Newman. $2,000

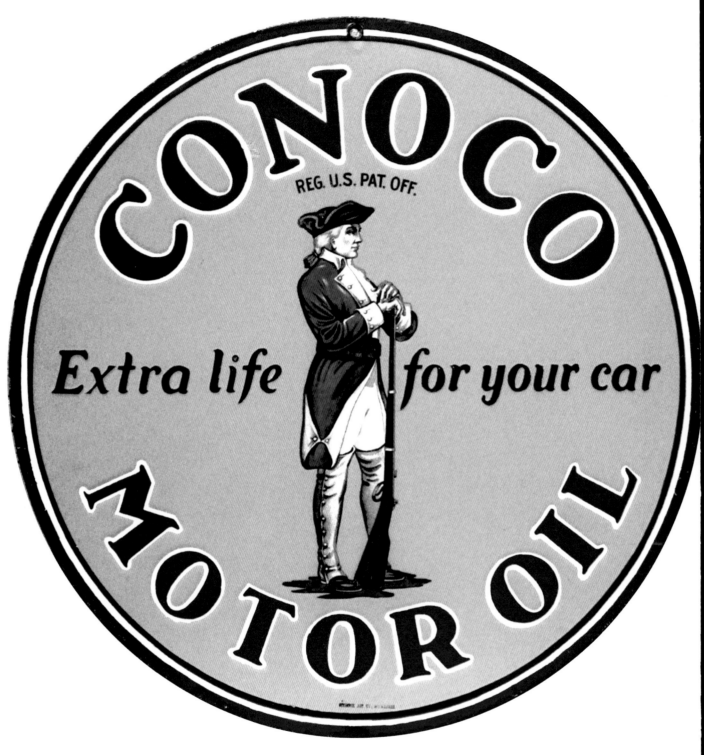

One of the most highly sought-after petroleum-related signs is shown here. This Conoco Motor Oil advertisement features their famous Continental Army soldier that was done with the decal process. Without a doubt the most unusual part of this sign is its remarkable condition. Although this sign was made in fairly prolific quantities, to find one in such condition as seen here is amazing. The ink stamping at the bottom center reads, "Reliance Advertising Company, Milwaukee." It measures 25" in diameter and dates from the 1920s.
Courtesy of Dennis Griffin. **$6,000**

Standard Oil Company's Red Crown brand gasoline was a well-known trade name in the industry and its familiar crown logo was one of the most recognizable petroleum company icons in the world. The 30" round example seen here was designed for use in a sidewalk stand. The fine print underneath the crown below the word "trademark" reads, "Patented October 12, 1915." A similar sign, without the blue detailing in the center, can be found in previous pages of the book.
Courtesy of Mick Hoover. $900

One more from a long list of advertisements for oil is this Vico Paraffin Base sign. It appears to date from around 1930 and measures 14" x 20".
Courtesy of Mick Hoover. $550

It is hard to say exactly where this Berryloid Service Station sign was used, though possibly at the local suppliers store. Again we see the dual use of the product being advertised by listing both automobiles and airplanes. It measures 22" square and dates from the 1920s.
Courtesy of Dennis Griffin. $2,000

Willard was a popular trade name in the automobile battery business during the 1920s. They spent thousands of dollars on advertisements to get their name in the public's mind. This two-color Batteries sign measures 18" square. *Courtesy of Mick Hoover.* $550

For years most telegraph companies relied on youthful messengers to scurry around town delivering and receiving messages. Although ADT is still in the public eye today, most people are not aware of its nineteenth century origins in the telegraph business. This advertisement probably dates to around 1900 as indicated by the style of bicycle that the telegraph messenger is riding. Notice that ADT wanted to promote that its messengers were "mounted." The sample seen here is a little rough around the edges, but like so many other rare advertisements, a better specimen may just never come along. *Private collection.* $1,600

Many of the major universities had their own agricultural farms and dairies. West Lafayette, Indiana, was home to Purdue University's Creamery. This die-cut milk bottle advertisement is somewhat unusual in the fact that it was designed to be displayed horizontally. Also unusual is its maker's mark, which indicates it was produced by a company called Kokon, possibly a manufacturer located in Kokomo, Indiana, but that is pure conjecture on my part. It measures 10" x 24" and dates to around 1930s. *Author's Collection.* $1,400

This Phenix Milk die-cut advertisement was produced in the 1930s. The graphics of an infant in a jumpsuit with an over-sized hat is somewhat reminiscent of the logo used by Arden Milk. It measures 24" x 10.5".
Courtesy of Dick and Diane Kinsey.
$1,200

Advertisers always seem to be able to come up with some way of placing everyday objects into their logo to help instill their company's image in our minds. Such is the case on this 35" x 18" Crescent Milk sign dating from the 1920s. The large yellow and white crescent moon jumps right out at even the most casual observer.
Private Collection. $600

The era of art deco makes a statement on this Midwest Ice Cream advertisement. Not knowing the company's exact location, one would think with a name like "Midwest" that a city such as St. Louis or Indianapolis would be the likely candidate for this company's home. However, looking at the image of the woman carrying the ice cream tray might indicate something that was produced in the south. It measures 30" x 20".
Courtesy of Dick Marrah. $600

This rare strip sign from Sunset Products dates from around 1930 and measures 6" x 30".
Courtesy of Mike Mihkelson. $5,500

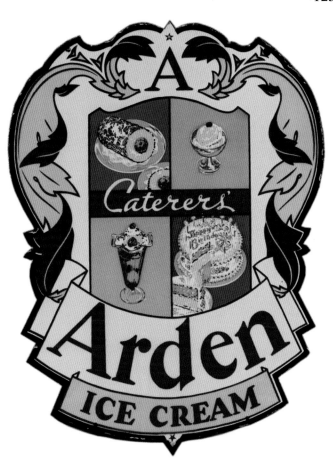

In the 1920s and 1930s many states began to promote tourism through public or privately founded associations. Michigan had its own such organization, which divided the state into regions. This advertisement is from the East Michigan Tourist Association and dates from the 1930s. It measures 18" x 14" and is ink stamped at the bottom right, "Burdick Enamel Sign Company, Chicago."
Courtesy of Rod Krupka. $550

This has to be the most spectacular sign produced by Arden Dairy. It is definitely a busy one with its multi-colored graphics. It dates from the 1930s and measures 37" x 28".
Courtesy of Dick Marrah. $3,500

In the 1930s Weyerhaeuser Corporation produced the 4 Square trade name. This round example measures approximately 24" in diameter.
Courtesy of Mick Hoover. $600

This Pawnee Ice Cream advertisement was designed to be suspended from an iron bracket. The product was sold in the Kansas City area in the 1930s. It measures 24" in diameter and is ink stamped at the bottom, "Veribrite Signs Chicago."
Courtesy of Dick Marrah. $500

Die-cut and early, this Long Wear Shoes advertisement was produced for the Craddock-Terry Company sometime around 1910. It carries the "Balto Enamel and Novel Company, Maryland" ink stamping at the bottom center. It measures 17" x 16" overall.
Courtesy of John Bobroff. $500

Many of the early motor oil producers touted the dual use versatility of their motor oils by incorporating aircraft into their sales pitch. The 20" x 32" Hi-V-I Motor Oil sign seen here is just such an example. It dates from around 1930.
Courtesy of Mick Hoover. $750

This is a very early advertisement from Goodrich. The first automobile tires incorporated a balloon-type design that is displayed on this sign. I'm not sure why they chose such dark colors for the leaf logo seen above the word "Goodrich." It appears that Goodrich borrowed Marathon Oil Company's slogan — "Best in the long run," although this may have come first. This is truly a historical item and a museum piece. It most likely dates from around 1910 to 1915. It measures 20" x 30". *Courtesy of Dennis Griffin.* **$3,500**

Appropriate graphics are the background on this Capitol Pale Lager Beer advertisement dating from the 1930s. It measures 16" x 24". *Courtesy of Bob Newman.* **$2,000**

Chapter Three:
Flanged Signs

All signs in this chapter were designed with a built-in side mount called a "flange." Normally, this amounts to no more than a ninety-degree bend on one edge of the sign. There are some other things that have shown up though, such as the "split flange" system used on some Western Union signs.

Many times the only damage to a sign will be limited to the flange area. Unless it is severe, this should not count heavily in the grading or the value of a sign. The face of a sign has the advertising — not the flange.

Be careful to inspect flat two-sided signs, as it may prove to have been a flanged sign that had the flange carefully cut off. Normally, small chips will follow the edge that the saw blade went along, and no porcelain will be evident along the edge as well.

This 24" x 19" Pocolene Motor Oil sign probably takes the prize for the largest Pennsylvania oil logo. Obviously the Pennsylvania 100% Pure Oil sign was placed front and center to help bolster sales. There is a large chip on the letter "R" that gives it the appearance of a letter "P." The Republic Oil Company produced Rocolene. It dates from the 1920s and is ink stamped near the bottom "Baltimore Enamel 200 Fifth Avenue New York."
***Courtesy of John Bobroff.* $650**

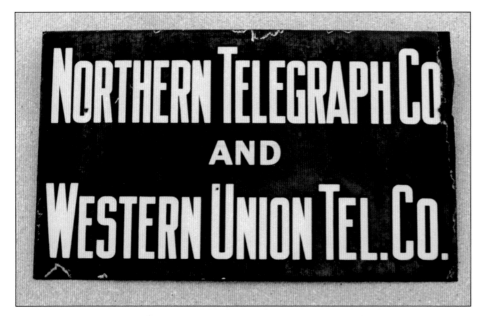

Similar in operation to the American Telegraph & Telephone Company, Western Union Telegraph Company had many cooperative leasing ventures with smaller companies. Northern Telegraph Company could be larger than regional in nature, but needed the national backing of a large telegraph company such as Western Union with its millions of miles of line. This advertisement measures 18" x 24" and dates from around 1915. It is ink stamped "Enamel Steel Sign Company Chicago."
***Courtesy of Mick Hoover.* $450**

Sherwin-Williams Paints produced one of the longest-lasting logos ever in the advertising world. Their familiar paint can spilling over the planet earth was a hit right from the start. Although this logo was produced over many years with tens of thousands of advertising pieces, the one seen here is more rare in its flanged form. It measures approximately 38" x 26" and dates from the 1920s. *Courtesy of Bob Newman.* $1,100

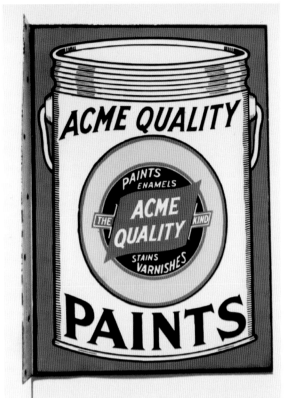

Paint manufacturers seemed to like putting their product container on their advertisements. Also, it appears the larger the better, as seen on this Acme Quality Paints sign dating from the 1920s. It measures 20" x 15" and is ink stamped, "B S Co. 188 North State Street, Chicago" and "Baltimore Enamel and Novelty Company, Maryland" on its flange. *Author's collection.* $800

No need to explain how this sign was used. The large word "Garage" at center does all the talking. It measures 18" overall and dates to the 1920s.
Courtesy of Mick Hoover. $550

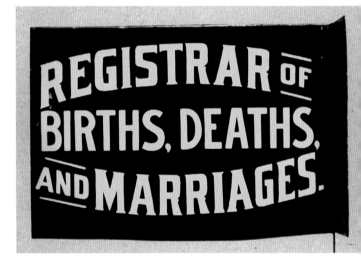

This unusual sign was most likely used at the county courthouse and tells its own story. It measures 12" x 18" and dates to around 1930. *Courtesy of Mick Hoover.* $400

I often look at an advertisement to try to make sense as to why a manufacturer decided on a particular theme. I would think that it would be better to add a third color instead of spending money by cluttering up the advertisement with dingbats and other miscellaneous eye catchers. But to each his own, and what is seen here is the final product. It was manufactured sometime around 1930 and measures 12" x 18". *Courtesy of Mick Hoover.* $400

With the huge amount of automobiles manufactured in the Detroit, Michigan, area there was bound to be a large manufacturing aftermarket to supplement the never-ending demand for parts and accessories. This oval Detroit Springs sign is an advertisement for just such a company. It measures 14" x 18" and dates from the late 1920s. *Courtesy of Mick Hoover.* $700

Here is another example of a major automobile tire manufacturer getting involved with other consumer products. I would suspect this sign was placed outside the local shoe store. It dates from around the 1930s and measures 18" x 20". *Courtesy of Bob Mewes.* $450

In the 1920s most automobile service stations did a fair amount of business from selling products other than petroleum. One such example is shown here on this Fisk Tires sign making it clear that auto supplies and their famous-brand tires were available as well as gasoline. It measures 18" x 24" and is ink stamped "Ingram-Richardson Beaver Falls Pennsylvania." *Courtesy of Mick Hoover.* $500

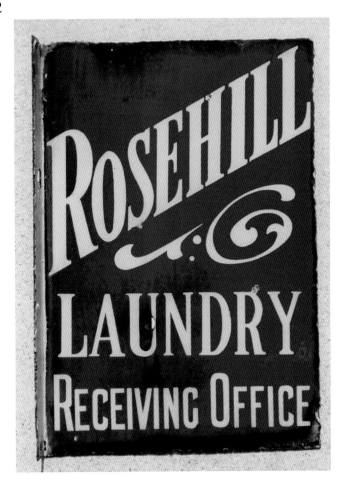

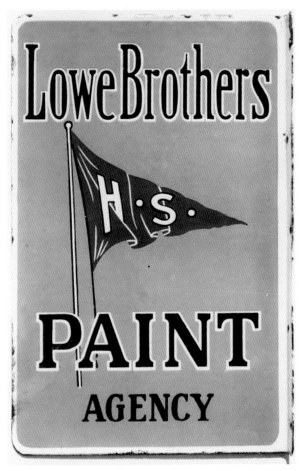

Depending on the size of the company this Rosehill Laundry Receiving Office sign could be one of a kind. It obviously was manufactured for use at a commercial laundry service. I'm not exactly sure what all that busy stuff is supposed to be underneath the Rosehill name. Most likely it's just "fill" that was commonly done in the early days to help get attention and take up dead space. This is an early one, probably dating to around 1905. It measures 20" x 14".
Private collection. $475

I've seen many Lowe Brothers Paint signs that are white on a blue background. However, I've never seen this color combination of white, blue, and tan. Not only are the colors more striking, but also the graphics are somewhat different leading me to believe that this was an earlier production sign than the more common blue and white advertisements. It has the "Ingram-Richardson, Beaver Falls, Pennsylvania" ink stamping at the bottom center. It measures 20" x 13".
Author's collection. $900

Great North Western Telegraph Company was a competitor of Western Union. Their lines ran throughout Canada. This advertisement was manufactured by Acton Burrows Ltd. of Toronto and measures 12" x 24". It dates from the 1920s.
Courtesy of Mick Hoover. $450

Michelin continues to be one of the largest producers of automobile tires in the world. This early advertisement probably dates to before 1920. Their whimsical tire man character, which became the hallmark for their advertising, has seen some changes through the years. The most notable one seen here is the smoking cigar. The sign measures 19" x 22".
Courtesy of Dennis Griffin. $1,600

The famous Gulf trademark is seen at the center of this No-Nox Motor Fuel advertisement. It measures 18" x 18" and dates from around 1930.
Private collection. $750

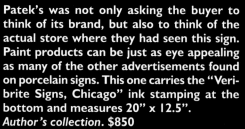

Patek's was not only asking the buyer to think of its brand, but also to think of the actual store where they had seen this sign. Paint products can be just as eye appealing as many of the other advertisements found on porcelain signs. This one carries the "Veri-brite Signs, Chicago" ink stamping at the bottom and measures 20" x 12.5". *Author's collection.* $850

The rear of a delivery wagon was the theme of this 25" x 20" North Western Fuel Company sign. It's just one more example of how graphics help sell a product or service. It's too bad the manufacturer couldn't have talked the head office at Northwestern Fuel into livening it up a bit with some color. That would have made it a knockout! The fine print on the wagon's axle reads, "Copyright 1911 by NW Fuel Co." *Courtesy of John Bobroff.* $525

Another advertisement targeting aftermarket sales is this one from Egyptian Lacquer Auto Refinishing. After this photograph was taken, the sign was professionally restored by Dawn and Terry Hubert (mostly Dawn – right, Terry?) and, I must say, looks spectacular. It measures 18" x 24" and dates from the late 1920s. *Courtesy of Rod Krupka.* $475

RPM was a national brand of motor oil produced in the 1920s. One can only guess as to what "Thermo-Charged" signifies. It measures 22" x 22".
Courtesy of Bob Newman. $900

The name Keen Kutter was a household word in tools and cutlery between the 1920s and 1950s. This larger-sized 27.5" x 18" advertisement shows their well-known logo. It dates from the 1920s.
Author's collection. $2,600

Although this Monogram Motor Lubricants sign was manufactured with only two colors, the scalloped edging gives it some pizzazz. It measures 18" overall and dates from the 1920s. It is ink stamped, "Balto Enamels New York."
Courtesy of Mick Hoover. $725

"Clean, Clear, Golden Texaco Motor Oil" was a highly successful slogan that could be found on dozens of different advertisements throughout the years. The die-cut sign seen here shows their multi-colored graphics of the pouring oilcan. It measures 23" x 18" and dates to around the late 1920s.
Author's collection. $1,800

Huyler's Candies produced this die-cut keyhole style advertisement in the 1920s. I can't imagine who thought up their slogan, as few people would need any encouragement to polish off a box of candies. It measures 8" x 20". *Courtesy of Bob Mewes.* $975

Another of the many independent telephone companies seen across America was advertised on this New State Telephone Company sign. Pay Station refers to it being a coin-operated phone. The most unusual feature of this sign is the red background color, which telephone companies stayed away from, as a rule. It measures approximately 12" x 18". *Courtesy of Mick Hoover.* $600

Many smaller telephone companies were licensed under American Telephone & Telegraph Company. This 22" x 18" Central Union Telephone Company advertisement is rare. It dates from around the 1920s. *Courtesy of Mick Hoover.* $750

Those of us familiar with the energetic character Reddy Kilowatt can see that his form on this sign is from his early years. Although this 16" x 18" advertisement has fairly thick porcelain, it probably dates from the late 1930s. *Courtesy of Bob Newman.* $1,100

Colorful, die-cut, and highly sought after by collectors, this **Wadhams Tempered Motor Oil** sign makes the grade. Its die-cut shape indicates its early manufacture, probably around 1915. It can also be found in one of my previous porcelain enamel encyclopedias as a flanged non-die-cut version, which is considerably less rare. It measures 24" x 18". *Courtesy of Bob Newman.* $2,500

This scarce Sunoco Motor Oil sign was manufactured in the 1920s. It measures 15" x 26".
Courtesy of Bob Newman. $1,300

Paint signs have gained in popularity over the years. Their general scarcity and use of vivid colors makes them quite collectible. Many manufacturers desired advertisements to feature their product. Such is the case with this Eagle Paint and Varnish Company's M.B.C. Mixed Paint sign. Take a moment and study the can and you will discover that the paint was actually named after M. B. Cochran, President of Eagle Paint and Varnish. It's so nice to be humble. It measures 12.5" x 11" and dates from around 1920.
Courtesy of Dick Marrah. $600

An unusual brand of cigarettes is seen on this advertisement dating from around 1910. It measures 7" x 16".
Courtesy of Bob Newman. $400

Like a piece of fine artwork, color selections are truly beauty in the eye of the beholder. With that in mind, I must say that the bright yellow band on this Mansion House Ice Cream sign wouldn't be my first choice to complement the plate of Neapolitan ice cream, but as long as they got the message across, who cares about color? This advertisement measures 14" x 18" and is most likely from the 1930s. *Courtesy of Dick Marrah.* $300

This is a variant on an otherwise identical sign that says "A Grade for Each Type of Motor" at the bottom. This one, with the Vacuum Oil Company wording, is much more scarce. It measures 16" x 24" and dates from the late 1920s. *Courtesy of Mick Hoover.* $700

Even the most sober production line personnel can occasionally have a bad day at the shop. This Postal Telegraph sign was made in large quantities in the 1930s as Postal Telegraph grew in size and stature. They were bought out in 1943 by Western Union. This larger sized advertisement shows just what can happen when quality control takes a vacation. The sign in the first picture presents itself well enough. However, upon turning the sign to the other side, it is obvious you would need to stand on your head for it to be legible. How such a major error could get by inspectors at the factory is almost beyond comprehension, but here it is in all its glory. It measures approximately 17" x 36".
Courtesy of Mick Hoover. $450

Massachusetts is known as the Bay State and is home to Wadsworth, Howland & Company. They produced a fairly large amount of advertising for their well-known Bay State Paints. Their cartoon-like puritan man can is at the center of attention on this 19" x 12" advertisement dating from the 1930s. *Courtesy of Bob Newman.* $700

In recent years a surge in popularity for items from the American west has made prices of certain advertisements skyrocket. This Auto Club of America sign was designated to be used in the region around Los Angeles, California. The large eagle featured as the center image gives plenty of impact to the viewer. It measures approximately 12" overall and dates to around 1920. *Courtesy of Dennis Griffin.* $1,900

Eveready was a huge manufacturer whose advertisements stretched beyond the American continent. Being an American-based company, it would seem as though they would advertise primarily in America, but their signs are quite rare here. In recent years there has been a barrage of Eveready signs coming from India. They feature a whimsical theatre usher, complete with uniform, walking down steps holding a giant flashlight. An example of one such sign can be found on page 88 of *More Porcelain Enamel Advertising*. When I was researching material for that volume in 1995, I believed this piece to have American origins. It was not until more recent times that this Eveready sign, along with hundreds of others, began their migration to America. The advertisement seen here is quite early, dating to around 1915, and features a large dry cell battery placed prominently on the sign. Ink stamping at the bottom center gives this piece away to being a product produced by Ingram-Richardson of Beaver Falls, Pennsylvania. It measures 10" x 15".
Courtesy of Bob Newman. $2,000

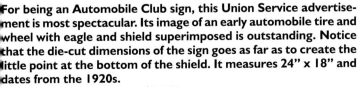

For being an Automobile Club sign, this Union Service advertisement is most spectacular. Its image of an early automobile tire and wheel with eagle and shield superimposed is outstanding. Notice that the die-cut dimensions of the sign goes as far as to create the little point at the bottom of the shield. It measures 24" x 18" and dates from the 1920s.
Courtesy of Dennis Griffin. $2,500

Similar in design to Goodyear's tire circling the globe design, this scarce U.S. Royal Cord Tires advertisement makes a huge visual impression. It was manufactured in the late 1920s and measures a large-sized 31" x 24".
Author's collection. $2,600

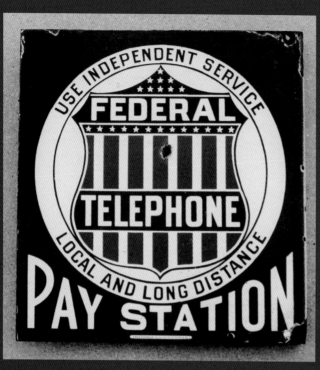

The Independent Telephone Corporation was the association for many of the smaller independent telephone companies that were competing with AT&T. Among these was Federal Telephone, whose advertisement is seen here. It measures 18" x 17" and is ink stamped at the bottom center, "Ingram-Richardson Beaver Falls, PA & 100 William St. N.Y."
Courtesy of Mick Hoover. $800

Looking at this rare advertisement one might wonder if there truly is going to be a horse-drawn stage pulling up to the depot. Although this sign is a relatively early one from around 1930, it was produced long after the era of horse-drawn transportation. Stagecoaches were the primary method of travel to areas the railroads did not reach in the days prior to automobiles. When buses began to replace stages, many of the early era buses continued to be known as stages even though there were no horses involved. Trona was a mining town in the Mojave Desert. It measures 15" x 17".
Courtesy of Dick Marrah. $1,400

GLIDDEN PAINTS
VERYWHERE ON EVERYTHING

Not wanting to be missed, Glidden Paints produced this die-cut arrow and target sign in the 1930s. If you look at its proportions, it's a wonder it didn't fly off its support bracket with the first strong breeze, as it has a weathervane shape and must have acted as such. It measures 15" x 29". *Courtesy of Bob Newman.* $600

GREYHOUND

Here is a somewhat unusual Greyhound sign. It most likely dates from the 1930s and measures 9" x 18". *Courtesy of Sue Gladden.* $450

This somewhat strange advertisement for a dye works company in Milwaukee, Wisconsin, was manufactured by F. E. Marsland as indicated by the ink stamping at bottom center. That's quite a selection of things that Otto Pietsch was involved with. The sign measures 12" x 22" and is apparently an early one, dating to around 1910. *Courtesy of Jeff Kaye.* $350

BRANCH OFFICE
OTTO PIETSCH
DYE WORKS
MILWAUKEE, WIS.
CLOTHING, FEATHERS, BLANKETS,
GLOVES, CURTAINS DYED AND CLEANED.

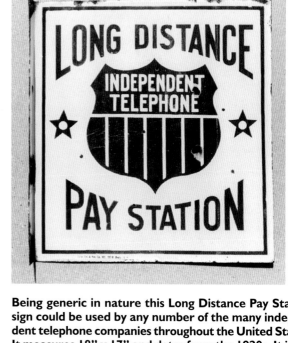

Here's a little cutie. Don't let this small-sized advertisement fool you. Quick Meal was one of the larger range manufacturers and produced plenty of other advertisements through the years. This die-cut flanged sign was manufactured around 1915. It measures 11.75" overall.
Private collection. $500

Being generic in nature this Long Distance Pay Station sign could be used by any number of the many independent telephone companies throughout the United States. It measures 18" x 17" and dates from the 1920s. It is ink stamped at the bottom left, "Balto Enamel & Novelty Co. Maryland 190 West Broadway New York."
Courtesy of Mick Hoover. $650

Marshall-Wells was a large manufacturer of hardware, cutlery and tools and was probably only second to Keen Kutter in name recognition. Their Zenith line of products is advertised on this 18" x 12" sign. Notice the multi-colored detailing that was done on the pinstriped framework around the sign's perimeter.
Author's collection. $1,200

The beautiful graphics on this Patton's Sun-Proof Paints sign are sure to make a lasting impression. Their famous sun logo shines brightly for all to see. It measures 26" x 18" and dates from around 1920. An almost identical variation can be seen in the chapter dealing with curved signs later in this book. It is ink stamped at the bottom center, "B S 166 North State Street Chicago and Beaver Falls Pennsylvania."
Author's collection. $3,000

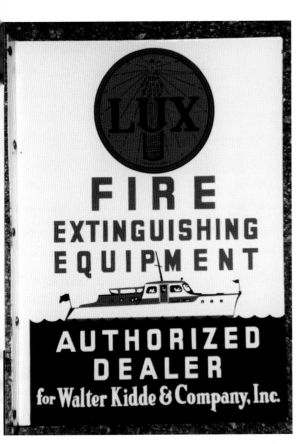

This American National Red Cross sign was originally manufactured without the Williamson County Chapter wording. These "blank" signs were produced in large quantities and distributed so that each local chapter could easily affix its name, which was applied with regular enamel paint using a stencil. It measures 11" x 14" and dates from around 1930.
Courtesy of Rod Krupka. $400

Although there is no mention of it, this 18" x 13" Lux Fire Extinguisher advertisement appears to be specifically targeted at the marine market. Walter Kidde & Company is still one of the largest manufacturers of fire extinguishing equipment to this day. It dates to the late 1930s.
Courtesy of Bob Newman. $1,000

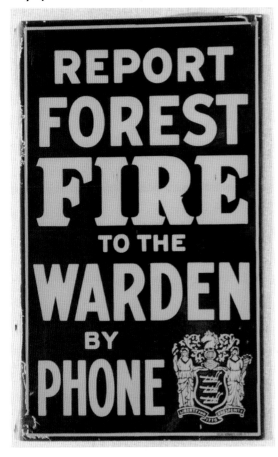

This 12" x 18" advertisement was manufactured for Duplate, an aftermarket supplier of automobile glass. It dates to the 1920s.
Courtesy of Mick Hoover. $600

This Forest Fire sign was designed and used specifically in the State of New Jersey. I have driven many of the back roads in that state and have found numerous signs identical to the one seen here still being posted. The majority of these signs were simply placed on trees near the roadside and most of my experiences have been seeing those signs almost completely overgrown by a tree consuming its porcelain advertising meal. The coat of arms at the bottom right is the state seal of New Jersey, the Garden State. The ink stamping below that reads: "Nelke Veribrite Signs New York." It measures 20" x 12" and dates to the 1930s.
Courtesy of Mick Hoover. $400

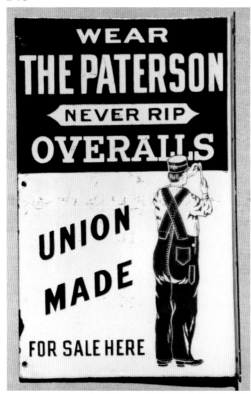

One of the smaller producers of overalls was Morotock Manufacturing Company of Danville, Virginia. This blue and white 10"x14" advertisement features the graphics of an American Indian representing their trade name overalls. Although it's difficult to see, the sign is ink stamped, "Balto Enamel & Novelty Co. Maryland" at the bottom right. It dates from the 1920s. *Courtesy of Jeff Kaye.* $2,200

Not the most prominent overalls manufacturer, but nevertheless one who knew how to order up a catchy sign was Patterson's Never Rip Overalls. This is an earlier one, most likely from around 1915. It measures 20" x 13" and carries the "Ingram-Richardson, Beaver Falls, Pennsylvania" ink stamp on the flange. *Courtesy of John Bobroff.* $1,000

One of the more unusual early telephone signs is this Pay Station example for Tri-County Telephone Company, which features a candlestick telephone in its triangular logo. It measures approximately 8" x 18" and dates from the 1920s. *Courtesy of Dennis and Jeanne Weber.* $1,200

A close-up photograph reveals the fine registration that is required to do a sign such as the Tri-County Telephone. As the photo suggests, it was manufactured with a stencil. *Courtesy of Dennis and Jeanne Weber.*

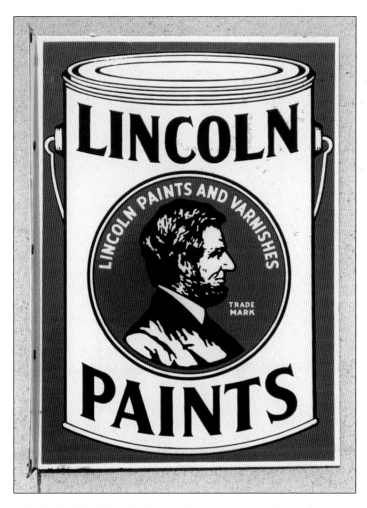

This 20" x 15" Lincoln Paints sign is rare insofar as its background is red. Most of these were manufactured with a green background. Like its green brother, it was produced in the 1920s, manufactured by Burdick Enamel Sign Company of Chicago and Baltimore.
Courtesy of Rick and Pamela Stevens. $1,200

Slight differences in the Sherwin-Williams Paints logo can be seen on this early 1920s advertisement. It measures 21" x 13".
Courtesy of Bob Newman. $800

Here is an advertisement for the Chicago Telephone Company. They were another in a long list of AT&T licensee phone companies connected with Bell System lines. One of the more unusual features to be noted is the white background, as few telephone signs deviated from blue. It measures 13" x 11" and dates from the 1920s.
Courtesy of Bob Newman. $800

I couldn't resist the opportunity to show you these five little gems from north of the border in Canada. For some reason American telephone companies shied away from signs this size and opted for the larger variety. Each measuring approximately 11" x 6", you wouldn't think they were very visible, but apparently they managed to be seen with little difficulty. AT&T discontinued the local and long distance telephone bell seen on the sign at left in the United States in 1921. However, Bell Telephone of Canada chose to continue its use well throughout the 1940s and I have actually seen these signs still in service as recently as a few years ago. The most notable of the group is without a doubt the Maritime Telephone & Telegraph Company Ltd. sign with its graphics of a candlestick telephone. Being a smaller company, this was also the most rare of the group. I would say the earliest date of production of any of these signs was probably around 1930.
Courtesy of Mick Hoover. Left to right: $300, $700, $250, $300, and $250

The large green clover graphics make this Penn Agency sign a standout. Considering the age of this piece, its condition is remarkable, as it appears to date from 1915. It measures 16" x 20".
Courtesy of Rick and Pamela Stevens. $1,600

I don't normally get too excited about signs that are just blue and white. However, I'm not the only one that seems to get wound up over this Breinig's Pure Paint sign. Obviously, its central graphics with a painter hanging precariously upside down on the top of a city steeple has a lot to do with its desirability. The careful placement of arched letters as well as choice usage of serifs makes this sign an eye catcher deluxe! It was manufactured by Ingram-Richardson as indicated by the ink stamping at the bottom center. It measures 20" x 12" and dates to around 1920.
Author's collection. $2,250

This Horse Shoe Tobacco sign is early, dating to before 1925. It was manufactured in fairly prolific quantities; however, this example is unusual as its condition is outstanding. It measures 8" x 18".
Courtesy of Rick and Pamela Stevens. **$650**

Somewhere in history between quilled and ballpoint pens, was a time when ink pens required a constant refill from a fountain. Normally fountains would be made of glass, and came in a variety of shapes and colors all with the common factor of being an inkwell to refill a fountain pen. I must admit that I am old enough to have used "fountain pens" when I was in elementary school. By this time inkwells were being replaced by a newer "cartridge" system, but even these were a mess to deal with, as I fondly remember coming home with ink spots on my hands and clothes many times. This 1915 example from Conklin's of Toledo, Ohio, shows prominently a line drawing of a man's hand reaching for one of its self-filling products. Talk about charisma! It measures 12.5" in diameter. *Author's collection.* **$2,300**

Chapter Four:
Curved Signs

This chapter contains signs that were designed to "go around" something. Normally this would be the corner of a building. This was quite common during the early part of the twentieth century. A special mounting bracket was employed to the corner of a building, and the sign fastened to the bracket. Curved signs had other uses as well, such as being found on telephone poles or streetlight posts. Some companies had their curved signs "tailor fit" to go right on the product being advertised. For example, a root beer sign to be fastened to a dispenser.

Like many Overalls advertisements, this gorgeous Carter's sign utilizes a railroad theme. Its blazing multicolored steam locomotive makes for plenty of action. This is an early sign and dates to around 1910. It measures 16" x 17" and is ink stamped "Ingram-Richardson Beaver Falls Pennsylvania" at the bottom right. *Courtesy of Bob Newman.* **$2,500**

Shoe repairing has been an occupation since antiquity. Today's craftsmen have modern equipment at their disposal and needed to advertise their ability to bring old shoes back to life. This beautiful vertical advertisement measures 48" x 12" and was manufactured sometime in the 1930s by Bob White Sign Company of Milwaukee, Wisconsin. *Author's collection.* **$1,400**

In earlier days many utility companies were experiencing constant problems with individuals who felt that utility poles were an appropriate place to get free advertising space. Such things as merchants who were having sales, community events, and a myriad of other local themes were put on paper and then nailed to utility poles for everyone to see. This problem continues to this day. Most of the time these impromptu advertisements would be mounted by the use of nails, making it a razor-sharp obstacle course for any lineman wishing to do their job. This die-cut bell-shaped advertisement was ordering the public to go elsewhere when looking for a convenient spot to post their announcements. It was manufactured by the Southern New England Telephone Company and dates back to around 1915. It measures 7" x 6".
Courtesy of Mick Hoover. $400

A lot of figural advertising was manufactured through the years, and of course some of this was made of porcelain enamel. This three-dimensional Emerson's Bromo Seltzer advertisement stands 39" tall and dates from the 1930s.
Courtesy of Jeff Kaye. $3,000

I feel sometimes a piece can be just as interesting on its reverse side. Seen here is how the factory produced the Bromo Seltzer die-cut bottle. Notice the reinforcing steel framework giving this heavy piece plenty of ability to be mounted safely.
Courtesy of Jeff Kaye.

St. Joseph, Missouri, was home to Wyeth Hardware & Manufacturing Company. This outstanding die-cut sign has the image of a very young driver, complete with goggles and cap, standing inside of three tires. Notice the different tread patterns on the tires. I'm not sure what the original guarantee was at the time, but I guarantee collectors would love to own it! It measures approximately 22" x 16" and dates to around 1920. *Courtesy of Dennis and Jeanne Weber.* $2,500

California Metal Enameling Company of Los Angeles, California, produced this early die-cut Bishops Chocolates sign sometime around 1910. It measures 16" overall. *Courtesy of Pete Keim.* $600

A shot of the backside of the Carhartt's curved sign. Notice all the woodwork involved in its manufacture. This sign could not have been in use for too many years, as the wood frame most likely could not have survived the elements to be in this condition. *Courtesy of Jeff Kaye.*

I can assure you that these Carhartt's Overalls signs are not growing on trees. Indeed, this is a most beautiful and unusual example of one of their advertisements. Although their famous railroad car superimposed on a heart is a familiar trademark, the wordy stuff going on in the rest of the sign is very unusual. Most notable may be the statement, "New Trade Mark to Prevent Fraud." Obviously there were unscrupulous manufacturers ready to imitate their well-known line. The sign measures 22" x 20" and dates to around 1910. *Courtesy of Jeff Kaye.* $3,000

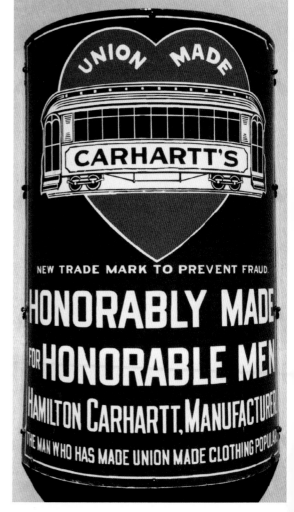

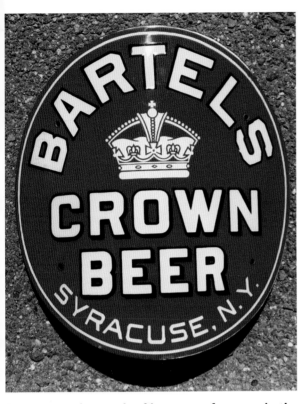

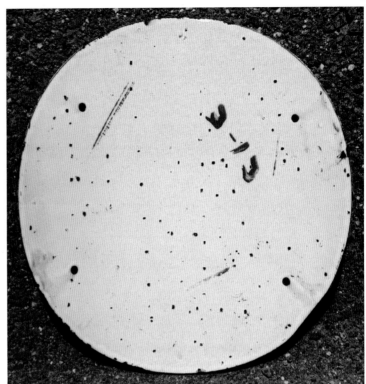

There were thousands of beer manufacturers in the United States prior to prohibition. This 15" x 14" advertisement is from Crown Beer of Syracuse, New York and dates from 1913.
Courtesy of Dick Marrah. **$500**

The reverse side of the Bartels beer sign reveals its true character. Along with a somewhat crude shape and early kiln markings, a very obvious "2-13" was finger scribed and fired into the porcelain revealing its February 1913 manufacturing date.
Courtesy of Dick Marrah.

Carhartt's produced this two-color curved sign sometime prior to 1920. Notice the play on words game that they achieved with the railroad car and heart. It measures 14" x 16".
Courtesy of Dick Marrah. **$1,500**

Not the best-known name in Overalls, this Bread Winner advertisement lets you know all the products that carried this trade name. It was manufactured by Baltimore Enamel & Novelty Company and is ink stamped at the bottom right. It measures 15" x 16" and appears to date from around 1915.
Courtesy of Bob Newman. **$1,000**

A striking advertisement for Eight Brothers Long Cut Tobacco. This outstanding sign was manufactured in the era when sweatshop tactics were beginning to give way to union shops. The nature of the advertisement lends itself to targeting primarily men — many of whom would look favorably upon the product being produced in a unionized plant, so the small "union label" notice near the bottom helped the public know that Eight Brothers was with them in the campaign against poor wages and working conditions. It measures approximately 22" x 14" and dates to around 1910.
Author's collection. $2,700

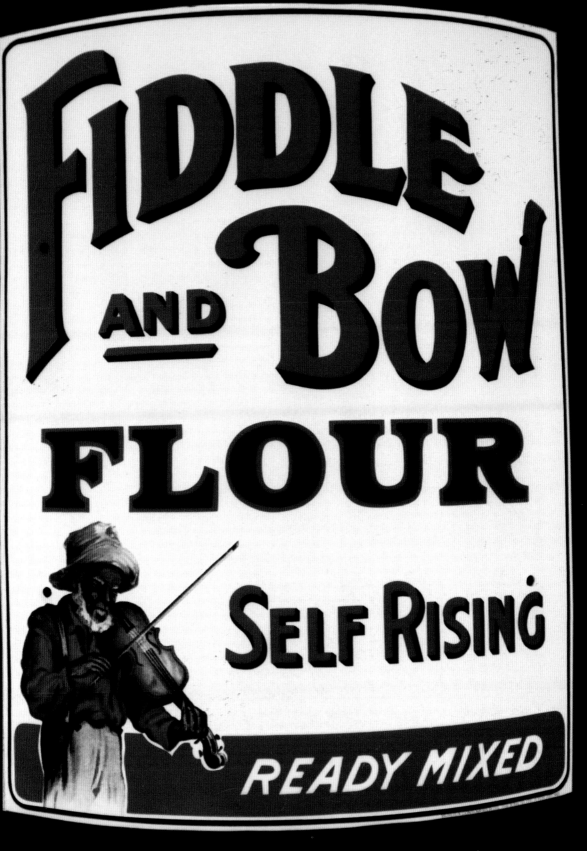

An absolute heart stopper is seen here. This historical Fiddle and Bow Flour sign was manufactured for Aunt Jemima Mills of Saint Joseph, Missouri, around 1915. This was one of four flour products that they produced in those early years. The others were Pied Piper, Red Top, and of course Aunt Jemima. The outstanding graphics of the man playing the fiddle at the bottom left puts this piece in a class by itself, at a price commensurate with its class! It measures 22" x 17".
Courtesy of Dick and Dianne Kinsey. $8,500

I wouldn't think of not giving you an opportunity to examine a close up of the Fiddle and Bow spokesman. His highly detailed colors and graphics were achieved by the process of firing a decal onto the sign. The end result – I am sure you will agree – is nothing short of spectacular. *Courtesy of Dick and Dianne Kinsey.*

Possibly for use on a visible gas pump, this Socony Gasoline sign measures 7.5" x 10.5" and dates from the 1920s. *Courtesy of Rod Krupka. $400*

A more traditional Carhartt's advertisement, this die-cut sign shows their famous railroad car design. The dark area in the bottom half is shadowing in the photograph from the sun. It measures 28" x 18" and dates to around 1910. *Courtesy of Jeff Kaye. $2,000*

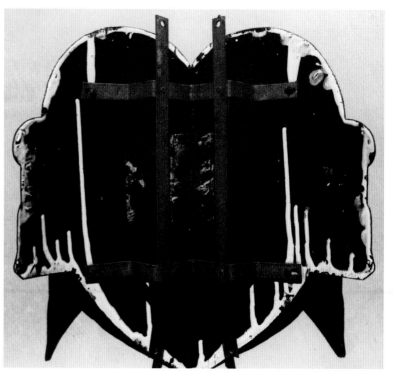

One should never get too used to looking at the reverse side of these old signs as the clues to its history may be revealed. This example is a winner with not only its original mounting brackets still intact, but also the thick gloppy white porcelain, which adds to its character. *Courtesy of Jeff Kaye.*

Almost identical to its cousin, which can be found in the chapter covering flanged signs, this die-cut curved Patton's Paints sign is outstanding. It was manufactured in the 1920s and measures approximately 28" x 18".
Courtesy of Rick and Pamela Stevens. $3,000

This beautiful Hilltop Bread advertisement features the likeness of a colonial woman as its central graphics. Its bright colors along with the additional word "Groceries" serving as a topper to the main body of the sign puts this piece as highly collectible. It measures 26" x 20" and is ink stamped at its bottom right, "Ingram-Richardson, Beaver Falls, Pennsylvania." *Author's collection.* $3,200

A scarce example of a Duck Head Overalls porcelain sign. This piece dates from around 1915 and is ink stamped "Ingram-Richardson Beaver Falls Pennsylvania" at its bottom center. Minus the bottom left corner, it is in super condition.
Courtesy of Bob Newman. $1,500

This Koester's Honey Bread sign has a convex shape, giving it a three-dimensional appearance. It measures approximately 15" in diameter and dates to the late 1920s. The small ink stamping at the bottom reads, "Baltimore Enamel 200 Fifth Avenue New York."
Courtesy of Rick and Pamela Stevens. $625

Chapter Five:
Pump plates, Lubester, & Petro signs

Many different kinds of gasoline have been manufactured through the years, each with their own trade name, that a separate chapter is appropriate to deal with some of the designs and companies that are found on pump signs, which are known in the hobby as "pump plates." A few of these are of a more common nature, produced in the thousands. Others are rare, with only a few examples known. Generally, the most difficult types of pump plates to obtain are from marine and aviation use. These were found at relatively few locations, and bring big bucks to sellers willing to part with these gems.

Also included in this chapter are those signs that were intended to be used on oil and grease dispensers — commonly called lubesters, along with a selection of miscellaneous petro advertising.

The bars and stripes logo used by Sinclair in its early years is seen on this 12" square oil pump plate dating from around 1920.
Courtesy of Mick Hoover. $1,150

Flying A produced this 10" square pump plate for use around 1950.
Courtesy of Mick Hoover. $350

Many petroleum manufacturers liked to advertise the high performance capabilities of their products. This Douglas Gasoline pump plate showed the consumer that their fuel has been Aviation Tested, although to what degree remains uncertain. The sign measures 12" square and appears to date from the 1940s.
Courtesy of Dennis Griffin. $800

A little newer one here. The familiar Union 76 logo is on this Unifuel Diesel Fuel sign dating from around 1960. It measures 11.5" x 9".
Courtesy of Rod Krupka. $300

Pan-Am was a trade name marketed by Standard Petroleum. The famous Standard logo is easily identified on this Quality Gasoline pump plate. Measuring 17" x 13", it dates from the 1950s.
Courtesy of Rod Krupka. $350

What appears to be two separate advertisements are actually part of the same deep blue porcelain sign. The trade names Viscoyl and Golden Tip were used by Viscoyl Oil Company of Louisville, Kentucky. The sign dates from the 1920s and measures 20" square.
Courtesy of John Bobroff. $750

This Midway pump plate dates from the 1930s. It measures 11" square.
Courtesy of Rod Krupka. $400

The outstanding graphics of the En-Ar-Co boy in checkered knickers are seen on this 8" round advertisement from the 1920s. It was most likely used on a crank bulk motor oil dispenser. *Courtesy of Bob Newman.* $1,200

A trio of pump plates is shown from B-A Gasoline. They measure 10" in diameter and date from around 1950s. *Courtesy of Rod Krupka.* $200 each

A scarce pump plate dating from the 1940s, this Platinum Plus Super Premium sign measures 13" x 12". *Courtesy of Gas Pump Ronnie.* $575

A more scarce pump plate, this Whiting Bros. 12" round example dates from the 1940s. *Courtesy of Rod Krupka.* $250

Another oil dispensing pump advertisement, this time from Socony Motor Oil. It lists the grade that was being dispensed as Light Medium. It measures 13" x 8" overall, including its mounting tab, and dates from the 1920s. It is two-sided. *Courtesy of Mick Hoover.* $600

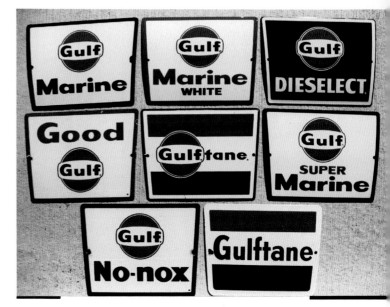

Here is a small four-sign grouping of pump plates from the Gulf Oil Corporation. Through the years there were others, but the ones pictured are from a more recent lineage, dating from around 1960. Each measures 10" in diameter.
Courtesy of Rod Krupka. $150 each

This veritable family reunion of pump plates will give you an idea as to some of the many products that were available during the 1950s and 1960s from Gulf Oil. Pricing these can be tricky, but a general rule of thumb is that advertisements that show the word "marine" or "aircraft" are normally more scarce and therefore of higher value. Each is not square but slightly die cut in the shape of a trapezoid, and measures approximately 9" x 11". The most common of these would fetch at least a $100 dollar bill and some of the Marine would probably be closer to $400 or more.
Courtesy of Rod Krupka. $100-400 plus

STOP YOUR MOTOR **Seaside** NO SMOKING

In the 1920s several of the better-known petroleum producers manufactured No Smoking strip-type signs. This one is from Seaside Petroleum and tells patrons to stop their motor, and more importantly, stop smoking. Measuring 6" x 36", it was designed to be hung from a bracket.
Courtesy of Dennis Griffin. $2,500

Here's a smaller sign possibly designed for use on an oil dispenser. It measures 6" in diameter and dates from the 1920s.
Courtesy of Bob Newman. $600

Mobil Oil's famous Pegasus logo is on this die-cut shield pump plate. It measures 13" x 12" overall. The small ink stamp at the bottom center reads, "Texlite Dallas."
Courtesy of Mick Hoover. $600

This brightly-colored H-C Gasoline pump plate was manufactured for use in the 1920s. It measures 14" square.
Courtesy of Mick Hoover. $700

A scarce Sunoco Mercury Made Motor Oil sign is shown here. The use of the winged caduceus at the top was relatively short lived. It measures 12" x 10". The ink stamping at the bottom reads, "Made in U.S.A. A553." It dates from the 1950s.
Courtesy of Mick Hoover. $500

A more scarce variation of a Sunoco Motor Oil plate is seen here with its familiar diamond logo encapsulating the word "distilled." Reserved specifically for its motor oils, the Distilled advertising was short lived, as it is rarely seen on any of their advertisements. It measures 12" x 10".
Courtesy of Mick Hoover. $400

El Paso Petroleum used this die-cut banner/torch combination on its pumps in the 1950s. It measures 10" x 11" overall. *Courtesy of Rod Krupka.* $400

The 1940s saw production of this Texaco die-cut pump advertisement. Its generic nature could give it the capability of being used on a variety of products. It measures 14" x 10" overall. *Courtesy of Mick Hoover.* $500

This Atlantic Premium pump plate features a street-side mounting pole graphic. It measures 11" x 13" and dates to the 1940s. *Courtesy of Mick Hoover.* $300

Here's a colorful eye-grabbing pump plate from E-Z Serve Gasoline. It measures 18" x 14" and dates from the 1950s. *Courtesy of John Collins.* $400

Quaker State continues to be a major supplier of motor oil to this day. Their famous Sterling Gasoline logo is on this pump plate dating from the 1930s. It measures 10" x 12".
Courtesy of Bob Newman. $600

This unusual die-cut Mobilgas advertisement measures 10" x 24" and dates from the 1930s. By looking at its side flange arrangement, it appears to have been mounted on a bulk fuel transport.
Courtesy of Mick Hoover. $450

Deep Rock had two separate colors, each for a specific grade of gasoline. However, which one is which remains a mystery. They measure 8.5" x 6" each and date from the 1940s.
Courtesy of Rod Krupka. $200 each

Some of the larger petroleum companies were eager to get their products distributed not only across the continent, but across the globe as well. Almost always the company's logo would appear on their advertisements that were designed for manufacture in foreign markets. Sometimes signs originating from a foreign country can be difficult to tell from its American counterparts, especially if that country's language is English. Such is the case on this 10" x 16" oval Mobiloil sign from the 1930s. Notice its not quite uniform shape and the inclusion of the words "Rochester U.S.A." at the bottom. This is an indication that the sign was produced for a foreign market by a foreign manufacturer, as no such signs have ever turned up for use in America. Signs like this one were made in copious quantities in such places as India and Africa, both of which used English to some extent as their language, and are finding their way into the American marketplace, en masse'. *Courtesy of Mick Hoover.* $450

Union Gasoline's shield logo grabs center stage on this 6" x 30" strip sign dating from the 1920s. *Courtesy of Dennis Griffin.* $2,500

The small die-cut lollipop-type shape of this Mobiloil Arctic sign was commonly used at oil dispensers in the 1920s. Although Mobiloil produced its fair share of porcelain enamel advertising to go with their products, most of the other manufacturers produced similar signs as well. It measures 11" x 9" overall and has two sides. The small print around the bottom perimeter reads, "This sign is the property of the Vacuum Oil Company and is licensed only on condition that the user guarantees to dispense from the container to which it is attached only genuine Gargoyle Mobiloil of the grade indicated." Obviously the old "bait and switch" has been with us a while! *Courtesy of Mick Hoover.* $500

This 18" x 12" Diesel Fuel 2 sign is the second from a grouping of three produced by Texaco. Also manufactured was the more common red and much more scarce yellow variants, which are not seen here. Like many porcelain signs of the relatively modern era, this one carries the ink stamp "Made in U.S.A." at the bottom right along with the proprietary date of "3.4.54" at the bottom left. *Courtesy of Rod Krupka.* $400

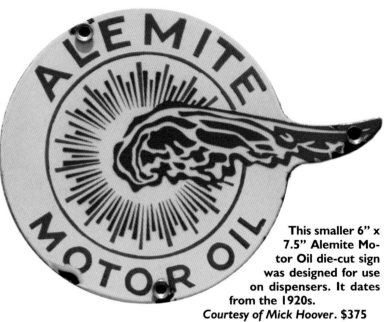

This smaller 6" x 7.5" Alemite Motor Oil die-cut sign was designed for use on dispensers. It dates from the 1920s.
Courtesy of Mick Hoover. $375

Although rarely ink stamped as such, Burdick Sign Company manufactured many of the pump plates that are so collectible today. This example from Humble Oil measures 18" x 11" and carries the Burdick ink stamp at bottom right along with the notation of its lesser-known supply house, "Tulsa." It dates from the 1940s.
Courtesy of Rod Krupka. $400

A first glance at this Texaco Motor Oil sign would indicate its lack of a proper mounting support, but a closer examination reveals that its die-cut shape includes a tab with two mounting holes at the bottom. This beautiful 5" diameter sign was used on oil racks and, as its black T logo suggests, dates from the 1920s. It's two-sided.
Courtesy of Bob Newman. $800

One of the more picturesque pump plates is seen on this 12" diameter Fortune Gasoline sign. The inclusion of the mythical god Mercury flying through the starry night holding a 1940s automobile gives this sign lots of desirability.
Courtesy of Bob Mewes. $1,200

Another beautiful No Smoking strip sign, this time from Hancock Petroleum. It's somewhat unusual insofar as there are only two mounting holes at the top, giving away the fact it was designed to be hung from a bracket. Like other strip signs, it measures 6" x 30". It is double-sided and features the famous Hancock logo as its central graphic. It dates from the 1920s.
Courtesy of Dennis Griffin. $3,000

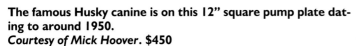

The famous Husky canine is on this 12" square pump plate dating to around 1950.
Courtesy of Mick Hoover. $450

One more example of a lubester advertisement, this Polarine Motor Oil sign tells the attendant to consult the chart for the correct grade. It measures 8" x 7" overall, including mounting tab, and is two-sided. Like some of the other lubester signs, this one lists the Standard Oil Company proprietary information around its bottom perimeter. It dates from the 1920s.
Courtesy of Mick Hoover. $600

A small-sized 2.25" x 8" Pennzoil strip sign is seen here. There's no mistaking that famous liberty bell graphic, which Pennzoil has used for many years. This one dates from the 1940s.
Courtesy of Bob Newman. $350

The Ethyl Corporation logo was placed on this Swifty Ethyl pump plate dating from the 1940s. It measures 10" x 12". Swifty is a mid-Ohio company and continues to do business to this day.
Courtesy of Rod Krupka. $400

A small-sized 5" x 7" plate from Sinclair featuring their familiar dinosaur logo. This one dates from the 1940s.
Courtesy of Bob Newman. $350

Chapter Six:
Municipal Signs

Most municipalities have created their own logo. These will normally incorporate some type of significant factor in the graphics, such as something that would be prominent to their area like a river, or farming, or certain buildings, or anything concerning the local history. Most of these types of signs were designed for the sides of municipal vehicles, therefore limiting their size to usually no more than 15" in diameter.

Although many municipalities used porcelain enamel signs throughout the years, it seems that there is a high concentration of these in the Pacific coastal states, most notably California.

The list seems endless and collector interest appears to have skyrocketed, as many of these local historical icons are in short supply to the collectors' market.

All of the municipal signs tried to incorporate images of things that were important locally in their graphics. No less than five items would be on the list for this City of Port Hueneme sign. Dating from the 1950s, it measures 10.5" in diameter.
Courtesy of Jeff Kaye. $350

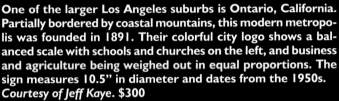

One of the larger Los Angeles suburbs is Ontario, California. Partially bordered by coastal mountains, this modern metropolis was founded in 1891. Their colorful city logo shows a balanced scale with schools and churches on the left, and business and agriculture being weighed out in equal proportions. The sign measures 10.5" in diameter and dates from the 1950s. *Courtesy of Jeff Kaye.* **$300**

Most of the municipal signs seen in this chapter feature attractive graphics. Following suit, the City of Indio had this 10.5" round sign produced for them in the 1950s. *Courtesy of Jeff Kaye.* **$250**

Although not technically a municipal sign, the similarity to other signs in this chapter warrant this advertisement's inclusion. The mountains throughout Southern California have been faithful providers of water through a series of canals. These manmade irrigation systems helped build the arid communities of the area, and have been crucial to the area's modernization for decades as seen in the November 6, 1912 date on this South Mesa Water Company sign. It measures 12" in diameter and dates from the 1950s. *Courtesy of Jeff Kaye.* **$200**

Like most of the other municipal signs found in this chapter, this piece was manufactured for use on city vehicles or signposts. It was actually produced for a county located in Northern California that features, in its central image, a large dam and reservoir with a coastal redwood in the foreground and a mountain, most likely Mount Shasta, in the background. It measures 12" in diameter and, like many others, found service in the 1950s. *Courtesy of Jeff Kaye.* **$200**

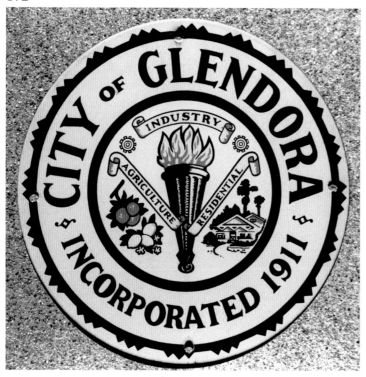

Manufactured for use in the 1950s is this City of Glendora sign that measures 10.5" in diameter.
Courtesy of Sue Gladden. $300

Located along the Colorado River on the edge of Eastern California is the City of Needles. Like most of the other municipal sign graphics, this die-cut shield sign gives an idea of what to expect in the vicinity — deserts, cactus, sagebrush, and the skull of an unfortunate steer. I'm getting thirsty! It measures 15" square and appears to date from thee 1940s.
Courtesy of Sue Gladden. $1,250

Eureka, California, is a coastal city located in the northern part of the state. Its municipal sign utilizes the great seal of the State of California. The human likeness with spear in hand may appear to be a Trojan warrior, but it is actually Minerva, the Roman goddess of wisdom. Dating from the 1950s, the sign measures 10.5" in diameter.
Courtesy of Jeff Kaye. $300

A slightly larger 10" diameter sign was used by Temple City for its municipal needs. It dates from the 1960s.
Courtesy of Dick and Diane Kinsey. $500

The City of Needles also produced signs for their municipal vehicles and other applications that were round. It is interesting to note the vast differences in the graphics from the previously-shown sign, giving one the impression that this must certainly be some other far away place in the world. This one measures 9" in diameter and dates from the 1950s. *Courtesy of Jeff Kaye.* $350

A silhouette of the State of California with a star appearing in its north central region designates the location of the City of Napa. Decades of wine production throughout the area has put it on the world map. Its three-colored diamond-shaped sign measures 9" x 15" and is from the 1940s. *Courtesy of Sue Gladden.* $300

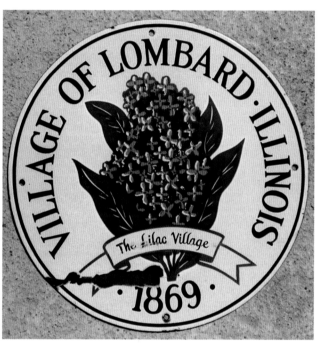

California wasn't the only state to use porcelain municipal signs, although apparently they were the most prolific. One such exception is this 12" diameter Lombard, Illinois, sign touting its Lilac Village. Although this municipality was incorporated in 1869, the sign probably dates to the 1950s. *Courtesy of Dick and Diane Kinsey.* $500

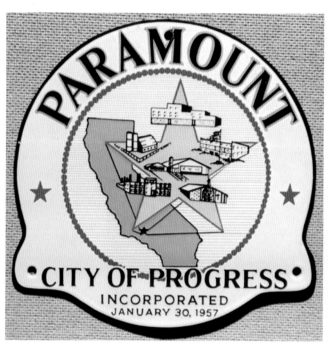

Paramount, California, proudly utilized this advertisement in the late 1950s through the 1960s. As with other municipal signs, its graphics incorporated some of the many varying industries and community contributors that formed the base of the town's infrastructure. It measures 8.5" overall. *Courtesy of John Bobroff.* $500.

Designed to welcome motorists to the city limits of El Monte, California, this 27" x 41" die-cut sign lists its population with a painted-on number. This could be changed occasionally as the need arose, still utilizing the original porcelain advertisement. Of interest on its central logo is the very 1950-ish insignia depicting a covered wagon and a futuristic "space rocket". *Courtesy of Jeff Kaye.* $600

The City of Roseville, California, utilized the appropriate graphics to depict an important part of their rich heritage on this 12" round sign dating from the 1950s.
Courtesy of Dick and Diane Kinsey. $625

Incorporated in 1850, the County of Santa Cruz is seen on this 9" diameter municipal sign.
Courtesy of John Bobroff. $500

Most likely designated for use on control trucks this Coachella Valley sign dates from the 1940s and measures 8" in diameter.
Courtesy of Jeff Kaye. $350

With a story to tell, this San Luis Obispo die-cut county sign measures 8.5" overall. It's most likely also from the 1950s.
Courtesy of Sue Gladden. $450

Collectibles with historical significance from the State of California seem to rank high with people who are seeking a part of the mystique of the Old West. This die-cut 4.5" Orange, California, sign dates from the 1920s and is quite rare. Its true-to-life size and beautiful graphics would put this sign on anyone's most-wanted list. Of interest is the unusual six mounting holes configuration that makes one wonder what could possibly require this much support on an item that only weighs approximately one pound. *Courtesy of Bob Newman.* $800

As usual, I wouldn't dare leave you without a photo of the reverse side of the Orange, California, sign. This original label is a clue that possibly this piece was never used in an exterior location or is new-old stock. Finding these types of labels is indeed a big deal, as they trace this piece of American history to its manufacturer, California Metal Enameling Company. *Courtesy of Bob Newman.*

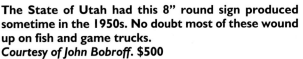

The State of Utah had this 8" round sign produced sometime in the 1950s. No doubt most of these wound up on fish and game trucks. *Courtesy of John Bobroff.* $500

Jefferson County, Colorado, had this 12" diameter sign made sometime around 1960. Many municipalities, even to this day, keep a mounted division ready to handle contingencies where a motor vehicle cannot go. *Courtesy of John Bobroff.* $750

Occasionally police and sheriff vehicles used porcelain signs as well. This one is from Pismo Beach, California. Dating from the 1940s, it measures 15.5" overall. Notice a mounting hole for each one of the star's points. That puppy's going nowhere!
Courtesy of John Bobroff. $550

Richmond, Virginia, used this die-cut sign in the 1950s. Adorned with an eagle at its top, it measures 14" overall. A closer look shows its ten-hole support arrangement. Talk about overkill!
Courtesy of John Bobroff. $500

The City of Buena Park put themselves on the map in 1953 with this 12" round sign showing some of the nearby cities and attractions in their graphics.
Courtesy of Jeff Kaye. $400

Portage, Wisconsin, was the home for this municipal sign dating from the 1950s. It measures 12" in diameter.
Courtesy of John Bobroff. $400

Incorporated in 1938, the City of Palm Springs, California, was a desert community that came into its own with highly touted golf courses, resorts, and other amenities. This 12" municipal sign was produced for use in the 1950s.
Courtesy of Jeff Kaye. $400

Produced for the City of Maywood, California, this 10.5" diameter sign was manufactured in the 1950s. *Courtesy of Jeff Kaye.* $300

1916 was the year of incorporation of the City of Monterey Park, California. This colorful 11" diameter sign was produced in the 1950s.
Courtesy of John Bobroff. $400

Few cities in America are as attached to the mystique of wealth as the City of Beverly Hills, California. Just one look at their municipal building pictured on the graphics of this sign will help convince you of its high-dollar heritage. It dates from the 1950s and measures 12" overall.
Courtesy of Jeff Kaye. $450

You could almost reach in and pick the orange featured on the graphics of this City of Covina, California, sign. Covina was incorporated in 1901. The sign measures 12" in diameter and, like many of the others, dates from the 1950s.
Courtesy of Jeff Kaye. $400

Situated around San Francisco is the County of Contra Costa. They produced this 10" diameter sign showing a mix of agriculture, shipping, and scenic beauty in the 1950s. Notice at the mountaintop the beacon with its rays pointing off in the distance.
Courtesy of John Bobroff. $400

The City of Pomona, California, was incorporated in 1888. The woman and cornucopia were there to show the abundance of agricultural wealth to be found in the area. However, I'm not sure why the dog. It measures 12" in diameter and dates from the 1950s.
Courtesy of John Bobroff. $400

In the extreme southern part of California about eight miles north of the Mexican border sits the town of El Centro. It's a desert community with a mix of industry and agriculture. I like the catchy slogan "Where the sun spends the winter." It measures 10.5" in diameter and dates from the 1950s.
Courtesy of John Bobroff. $250.

Ventura County, California, produced this sign for use on its fire vehicles. Measuring 7" in diameter, it dates from the 1940s.
Courtesy of Jeff Kaye. $300

The San Francisco Bay Area was the location of Hayward, California. The modernistic logo used at its center made the typical representations. The town is an older one, incorporated in 1876. It measures 10" in diameter. *Courtesy of John Bobroff.* $250

Sharing similar forms of prosperity with California towns is Fort Morgan, Colorado. A rich history of mining and agriculture as well as the territory's original military fort is depicted on this sign's center graphics. It measures 10.5" in diameter and dates to the 1950s. *Courtesy of Dick and Diane Kinsey.* $400

Here's an eye catcher! This relatively recent vintage Sevier Sheriff's sign was utilized in their Jeep Posse. I can't say I've ever seen anything quite like this. It measures 9" in diameter and was most likely affixed to the sides of Jeeps. Notice that the convenient mounting holes were located at the ends of the star. *Courtesy of John Bobroff.* $300

Like many other municipalities, agriculture plays an important role in the daily life of the City of Lodi, California, as seen on this 10" round example dating from the 1950s. *Courtesy of Dick and Diane Kinsey.* $650

Chapter Seven:
Thermometers, Door pushes, Match strikers, & License plate tags

I've consolidated four smaller categories into this chapter to help streamline the book. Within this chapter the many door pushes that can be seen gives credence to their relatively low cost to produce combined with placement at such high-visible areas as general stores, cafés, and railroad stations.

Similar in design, but much more scarce are the match strikers with advertising that is universally smaller-sized, comparatively speaking.

Thermometers, of course, were a popular way to reach the general public's eye and will be seen in an assortment of sizes and products being advertised, with the added attraction of letting the public keep tabs on the weather.

Also within this chapter is a small inclusion of license plate tags. These were designed to be attachments to a vehicle's license plate area in the early years of the automobile. Again, an assortment of advertisements can be found, but mostly they seem to stay focused on automobile-related subjects. Many of these used the delicate cloisonné manufacturing process. Others were stenciled or silk-screened. Those without listed dimensions are similar in size to the others, normally 3" to 5" overall.

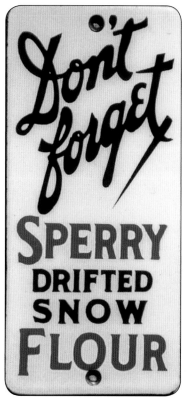

Probably dating from the 1920s, this 7" x 3.5" Sperry Flour sign incorporates some script letters in its graphics.
Courtesy of Dick and Diane Kinsey. $625

This Fleischmann's Yeast door push was manufactured in a small 4" x 3" size. This is about as small as you could expect for a door push that could still get the message across. It dates to around 1915.
Courtesy of Dick and Diane Kinsey. $350

A rarely seen example of a Bullshead Ginger Ale door push is featured here. Condition is everything and this piece is as good as it gets. It measures 4" in diameter and, I believe, dates to sometime around 1930.
Courtesy of Dick and Diane Kinsey. $600

One in a never-ending procession of advertisements manufactured by the soft drink giant, Coca-Cola, this one is a full span door push mounted at the left and right sides of the door's frame. This not only gave more protection against abuse when opening and closing a door, but gave the manufacturer an excuse to increase sales by increasing the size of the advertising. These die-cut full span door pushes became popular in the 1940s and were manufactured prolifically. They seem to have especially caught on in Canada, although this example looks to be as American as apple pie. It measures 4.5" x 29". *Courtesy of Bob Newman.* $600

Sometimes where a product gets its name never becomes apparent until the obvious is put in front of us. At least for me, the household word "Palmolive" was just another trade name until this little door push came along. Makes sense to me! Measures 6.5" x 4" and dates to around 1915. *Courtesy of Bob Newman.* $1,200

Here's one manufactured around 1915 for Crystal White Soap. That's a lot of bubbles! It measures 8.5" x 4". *Courtesy of Dick and Diane Kinsey.* $500

Hills Bros. manufactured several varieties of similar appearing thermometers in the era around 1920. This 21" x 9" variant says "Particular People Prefer Packages" at the bottom.
Courtesy of Bob Newman. $900

This scant 3.25" diameter thermometer uses a porcelain dial for its advertising. It was manufactured in Connecticut most likely in the 1920s.
Courtesy of Bob Newman. $450

Dating from the 1930s this two-color door push features an image of its manufacturing facility and measures 6" x 4".
Courtesy of Dick and Diane Kinsey.
$250

The rarity and high demand for this Orange Crush match striker makes it highly desirable. It dates to around 1930 and measures a scant 5.5" x 3.5".
Courtesy of Dick and Diane Kinsey. $900

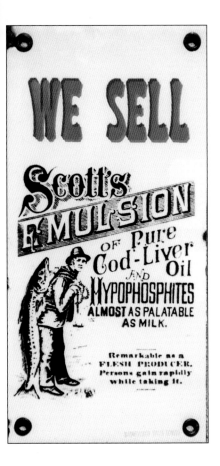

Smaller sizes normally prevents most door pushes from including much wording or graphics. This Scott's Emulsion door push is the rare exception. Although it's difficult to pinpoint its exact age, and even though it doesn't promise to cure anything, I believe it dates prior to the Pure Foods and Drug Act of 1906. A complete read of the product's claims seem to be somewhat conflicting; at the bottom the manufacturer states people will gain rapidly while taking it, although apparently it was made from cod-liver oil, which no doubt acted more like a laxative. Regardless, it's a phenomenal piece of porcelain American history. It measures 9" x 4.5".
Courtesy of Dick and Diane Kinsey. $1,350

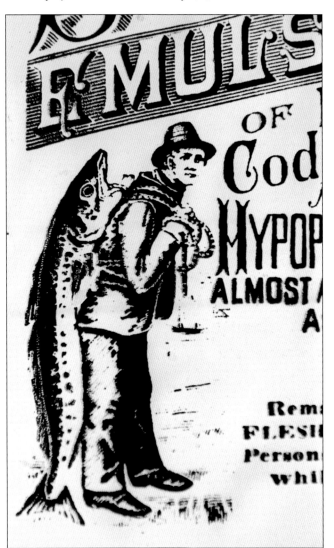

A close-up of the beautiful graphics on the Scott's Emulsion door push is in order. Although only done in two colors, the attention to fine detail seen on this historic piece is reminiscent of the technical abilities of someone working at the Bureau of Engraving and Printing as noted by the fine lines going through the word "Emulsion" above the fisherman. If you look closely, there is a ship at sea near the waist of the man holding the fish. A gem!
Courtesy of Dick and Diane Kinsey.

Still another close-up is in order to show you the rare "Stonehouse Signs – Denver" ink stamping. Although not one of the more prolific manufacturers in America, Stonehouse Signs left its mark on American advertising in the early years of the art.
Courtesy of Dick and Diane Kinsey.

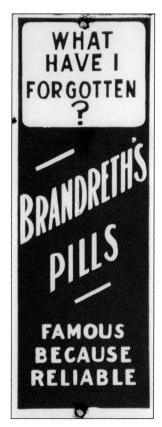

Capitalizing on shoppers' lack of memory seems to be the theme of this Brandreth's Pills door push from around 1915. Its tall rectangular shape is unusual, measuring 8" x 3". *Courtesy of Dick and Diane Kinsey.* $525

A three-color advertisement for Kirk American Family Soap measures 8.5" x 4" and dates from around 1910. *Courtesy of Dick and Diane Kinsey.* $600

Listerine was already a major player in the oral hygiene market in the 1930s. Their advertisement for toothpaste was manufactured with a silk screen. It measures 11" x 4". *Courtesy of Jeff Kaye.* $500

A rarely seen advertisement for Keystone Cigars is featured on this 6" x 4.5" door push dating from around 1920. *Courtesy of Pete Keim.* $450

Here's one that gets a lot of people wound up. Inclusion of the bear in the graphics of this Polar Tobacco door push makes it an eye-catching and highly-desirable advertisement. It measures 6" x 4" and dates to around 1910. *Courtesy of Pete Keim.* $800

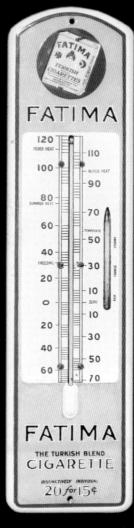

One of the more popular brands of cigarettes in the 1930s can be seen on this 27" x 7" thermometer. Turkish Blend Cigarettes were in vogue during that period, with many of their manufacturers using highly-graphic advertising to help sell their products. This unusual example features not only a thermometer, but also a change in weather indicator to its right. Most likely this functioned similar to a barometer, as it measured some type of atmospheric pressure. *Courtesy of Rick and Pamela Stevens.* $800

A fairly popular brand for consumers was Magic Yeast. This early company had this door push manufactured sometime around 1910. It measures 6" x 3".
Courtesy of Dick and Diane Kinsey. $750

Not to be confused with its twin, Magic Yeast door push, this Yeast Foam door push was manufactured in the same 5" x 3" size and color/graphic pattern. It dates from around 1915. *Courtesy of Dick and Diane Kinsey.* $400

A close-up of the package graphics shows lots of detailing. The entire thermometer minus the package was done with a stencil, but the black areas on the package box were done with a silk screen—this being the only way to give satisfactory results on a fairly high production item.
Courtesy of Mick Hoover.

Nature's Remedy was one of America's best known laxative products. Their early years incorporated designs of several similar thermometers that were all slightly different but still focused on product sales. I believe this to be one of the earlier ones, from the 1920s. It's unusual insofar as its left side lists the radiator alcohol percentages necessary to prevent freezing the cooling system of an automobile. It measures 27" x 7". *Courtesy of Mick Hoover.* $550

Ex-Lax was another advertiser that had several similar variants manufactured in the way of thermometers. This unusual example features a horizontally-mounted thermometer, as can be seen at the upper center. It measures 36" x 8" and dates from the 1940s. It has edges that are bent around the thermometer approximately one inch giving it a box-like appearance when mounted in position on site. *Courtesy of Bob Newman. $600*

There always seems to be an unending stream of surprises when going through the many variations of porcelain advertisements. This thermometer is unusual, partly because of its unconventional size of 35" x 5". It was also manufactured by Taylor, which made relatively few advertising thermometers, but most of its uniqueness comes from the fact it is advertising both Standard Oil Company and Mobil Company products at the same time, even though they were competitors. It appears to date from the 1940s. *Courtesy of Bob Newman. $800*

Our Canadian neighbors to the north produced thousands of porcelain enamel advertisements through the years. Many of these were bilingual in nature and included French. In addition, many of the American manufacturers sought out Canadian customers as a successful addition to their advertising and marketing. Such is the case on this Canadian Orange Crush thermometer. It measures 15" x 6" and appears to date from the 1940s. *Courtesy of Dick and Diane Kinsey. $575*

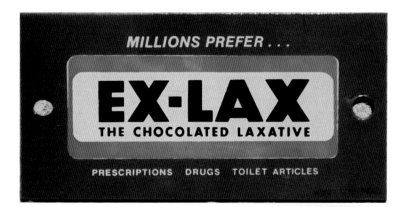

Obviously intended for use on the entrance to a drugstore, this Ex-Lax advertisement lists some of the sundry items to be found when one passes through the door. Its flat design would place its manufacturing date to the 1930s or later. It measures 3.5" x 7" and is ink stamped at the bottom right "Veribrite Signs Chicago." *Courtesy of Dick and Diane Kinsey. $425*

Counterfeit cigar manufacturing must have been big business in the early 1900s, as Pharaoh Cigars tries to warn the public how to spot the genuine article. This two-color 6" x 4" advertisement is enhanced by the use of a match striker on its surface. It dates from around 1910. *Courtesy of Pete Keim. $475*

Although similar in design to some of its advertising cousins, this Hills Bros. thermometer is uniquely different. It carries the words "Red Can" at the bottom, which is seldom seen on their thermometers. It has the usual "patent March 16th, 1915 Beach Coschocton, Ohio" ink stamping, measures 21" x 9", and was manufactured in the 1920s.
Courtesy of Dick Marrah. $800

Hills Bros. manufactured at least three different styles of porcelain enamel thermometers in their early years. This similar-looking door push is much more scarce. I believe it to date to around 1920 and it measures 8" x 3.5". The ink stamping at bottom left reads, "Registered U.S. Patent Office."
Courtesy of Dick and Diane Kinsey. $1,525

A close-up reveals the wonderful attention to detail found on the Recruit Little Cigars graphics. *Courtesy of Dick and Diane Kinsey.*

Like many of the advertisements dating from around 1915, this Recruit Little Cigars door push is exceptional. Similar in nature to some of the other early graphics, the central image of this door push was done with a fired-on decal allowing for a high degree of intricacy in the design. It measures 9" x 4". *Courtesy of Dick and Diane Kinsey.* $2,200

Sometime around 1940 this NuGrape Soda advertisement adorned the entrance of a store. Measuring 6" x 12", it was manufactured by Texlite. *Courtesy of Sue Gladden.* $425

Dating from the 1940s, this Wishing Well Soda advertisement shows an image of its swirled glass container and measures 11.5" x 4". *Courtesy of Dick and Diane Kinsey.* $500

This unusual 9" x 4" door push had its own built-in handle. Betsy Ross was a popular brand of bread in the 1930s. *Courtesy of Dick and Diane Kinsey.* $525

What a magnificent example of early American porcelain advertising! All the central graphics included on the package were done with a fired-on decal. This is truly a testimonial to the manufacturer's art. The multi-color detailing is precise and reveals the smallest attention to fine artwork such as the ox team pulling a plow in the background near the man's arm. The ink stamping "D 6439" at bottom right is a new one to me. It's hard to believe these pieces would be serial numbered, and such a high designation would unlikely be from a production style or job number. Measuring 6.5" x 4", it appears to date from 1910. *Courtesy of Dick and Diane Kinsey.* $3,000

This rare example of a Five Hearts Cigar door push measures 6.5" x 4" and appears to date from around 1910. *Courtesy of Pete Keim.* $500

Union Made was the sign of the times in the early twentieth century. Feifer's took their place in a long list of cigar manufacturers on this 3" x 21" strip sign door push. I believe it was manufactured around 1915. *Courtesy of Pete Keim.* $450

Another example of a match striker is seen on this J.H.P. Five Cent Cigar advertisement. I believe it to be an early one, likely dating from around 1905. It measures 6" x 4". *Courtesy of Pete Keim.* $350

These two photographs give some idea as to the busy nature of the Lay or Bust thermometer. Of particular interest is the wording that promises a thermometer in exchange for empty bags. Sounds like a deal to me!
Courtesy of Jeff Kaye.

More than a casual glance is required to discover all the busy graphics on this Lay or Bust Feeds thermometer dating from the 1930s. It measures 20" x 7".
Courtesy of Jeff Kaye. $1,200

The proportion of the grommet holes compared to the overall size of this advertisement should give an indication of its 3" x 4" dimensions. As can be figured by the notation at the top, a dime goes a long way! It dates from around 1910. *Courtesy of Dick and Diane Kinsey.* $350

This die-cut Red Rose Tea door push utilizes a red, white, and green color scheme. One of the more prolific brands of tea in America, this advertisement dates from around 1930 and measures 9" x 3". *Courtesy of Dick and Diane Kinsey.* $425

Here's an 11" x 4" four-color graphic advertisement for Pro-phy-lac-tic Perma Grip Toothbrushes. It probably dates from the 1930s. *Courtesy of Pete Keim.* $400

Of particular interest to those who collect petroleum-related products is this rare Sunset Oil Company thermometer. It measures a scant 3" in diameter and dates from the 1920s. As you can see, it's still giving an accurate reading of the temperature as I was photographing in the Southern California heat in the wintertime. *Courtesy of Bob Newman.* $500

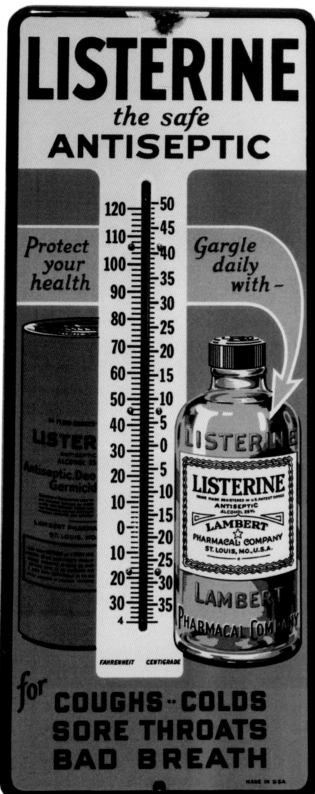

Based on a railroad theme, Pay Car Chewing Tobacco is featured on this 6" x 3" advertisement dating to around 1905.
Courtesy of Dick and Diane Kinsey. $550

A major player in the hygiene market is Listerine Mouthwash. This early advertisement shows their product with its bottle and protective packaging. Measuring 30" x 12", it probably dates to around 1930.
Courtesy of Jeff Kaye. $1,500

A photograph of the backside of the Listerine thermometer reveals the unusual mounting hole configuration. Most likely this was done to adjust the height of the thermometer.
Courtesy of Jeff Kaye.

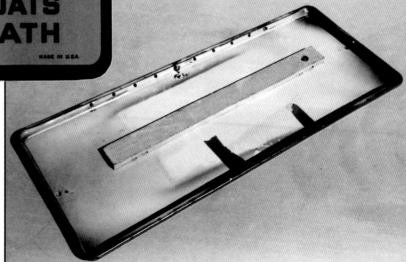

The early days of automobile touring required careful planning and the use of available guide books. One such tour book was the *Red Book Automobile Guide*. Their advertisement appears on this early 1920 match striker. It measures 6" x 4" and is ink stamped "Baltimore Enamel and Novelty Company" on its reverse side. *Courtesy of Mick Hoover.* $500

Dating from around 1920 is this 6.5" x 3.5" advertisement for Rain Water Crystals. *Courtesy of Pete Keim.* $300

Most likely Canadian in origin, this early Royal Yeast Cakes door push appears to have been manufactured with a silk screen. It measures 6" x 3" and dates to around 1905. Notice the "Toronto & Chicago" notation at the bottom of the can. *Courtesy of Pete Keim.* $500

Even though one of these Coca-Cola die-cut thermometers was pictured in one of my previous Porcelain Enamel Advertising books, I thought you might like the opportunity to see all four variants in one group shot. Obviously, the two at left are in French and originated from Canada. They all measure 18" x 5.5" and date to around the 1940s. *Courtesy of Bob Newman.* $1,000, $1,000, $1,500, $1,200

This outstanding Case eagle door push dates from around the 1920s. It measures 16" x 6.5", and must have found use at implement dealerships.
Courtesy of Dick and Diane Kinsey. $1,175

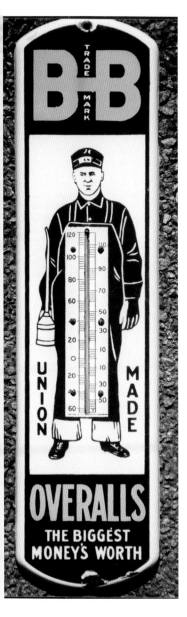

Large graphics of a railroad engineman were used to create the maximum impact on this B-B Overalls porcelain thermometer. It measures 27" x 8" and dates to the 1920s. *Courtesy of Bob Newman.* $1,200

Winchester Roller Mills was a regional flour mill located in Winchester, Kentucky. It appears the Smith P. Kerr Company was bought out by McEeldowney, Matlack & Woolcott sometime in the early 1900s as evidenced by the inscription on the lower portion of the graphics. Although rarely done in this day and age, it was common a hundred years ago to list the precursor company on advertisements when a manufacturer changed hands. Although only two colors, the flour sack graphics make a considerable improvement to the eye appeal of this early advertisement. It measures 6" x 3" and probably dates to around 195. *Courtesy of Pete Keim.* $825

Apparently most anything can show up on a door push. This unusual example, from the 1920s, measures 6" x 3.5". Better brush afterwards! *Courtesy of Pete Keim.* $400

A fired-on decal was used to obtain the central image on this O'Sullivan's Heels door push. It measures 9" x 4.5" and probably dates to 1920. *Courtesy of Dick Marrah.* $500

This advertisement for Langendorf Bread measures 7" x 3.5" and dates from around 1915. *Courtesy of Pete Keim.* $350

Unlike its plain looking cousin, the two Northwestern Yeast Company advertisements seen here are a graphic reminder of the possibilities to be found in early advertisements. Both of these door pushes were manufactured around the same time and feature products manufactured by the same company. Magic Yeast and Yeast Foam were household names in baking during that era. Like some of the other graphic door pushes, the images to create the boxes of products were done with a fired-on decal giving a high degree of detail. They both measure 6" x 3" and most likely date to around 1905. *Courtesy of Pete Keim.* $950 each

The 1930s saw this American Pharmacist oval door push in use. It measures 3" x 4.5". *Courtesy of Dick and Diane Kinsey.* $450

Although this Carhartts Overalls door push seems to be manufactured in the 1930s, its quality would not indicate being produced by one of the larger manufacturers. It measures 7" x 3.5". *Courtesy of John Bobroff.* $250

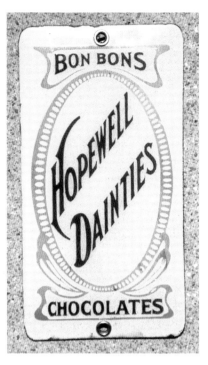

Bon Bons is a household word in the candy business to this day. This advertisement dating from around 1920 shows their Hopewell Dainties line of products. It measures 6" x 3.5".
Courtesy of Pete Keim. **$450**

Simple in design but scarce is this Wilbur Chocolates door push. It measures 5" square and dates to around the 1920s. *Courtesy of Pete Keim.* **$300**

Here's a matched pair from Coca-Cola. They appear to date from around 1940 and were meant to be given away to retailers who sold Coca-Cola products. Their logo is placed prominently, leaving little chance to not be seen. They measure 8" x 4" each.
Courtesy of Bob Newman. **$800 each**

This rare and colorful Jests advertisement dates from 1940. The inclusion of the multi-colored graphics was a smart decision on the part of the advertiser as it brought this door push to life. Just what is a "sour stomach?" It measures 8" x 4".
Courtesy of Dick and Diane Kinsey. **$2,000**

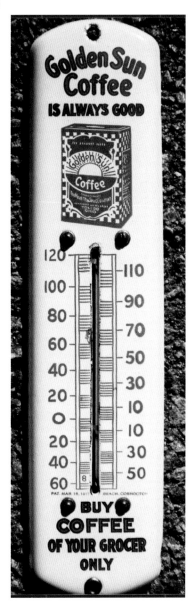

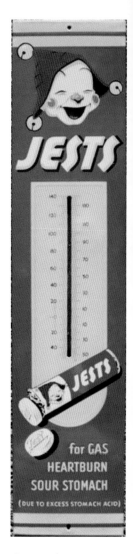

Beach, of Coshocton, Ohio, normally manufactured larger-sized advertising thermometers. This smaller 11" x 3" version was produced for Golden Sun Coffee in the 1920s. Of interest is the wording at the bottom, asking the consumer to buy coffee from only their grocer. Where else would anyone go?
Courtesy of Bob Newman. $650

What a gorgeous little piece of American advertising! This Rex Tobacco door push, dating from around 1910, used a decal for the image of the tobacco package. Measuring 7" x 4", its beauty is only matched by its magnificent condition.
Courtesy of Bob Newman. $1,200

A rare thermometer with outstanding graphics is seen here on this Jests advertisement dating to around 1950. It measures 36" x 8".
Courtesy of Bob Newman. $2,500

One of possibly two known, this Coca-Cola door mounted advertisement is actually a "door pull." Its stylish handle is original and helps date this rare piece to around the late 1930s. It measures 10" x 2.5".
Courtesy of Bob Newman. $2,000

Here's that famous Orange Crush logo, this time on a 5" round advertisement dating from the 1930s. *Courtesy of Dick and Diane Kinsey.* **$900**

An example of a superb image that was not done with a decal. Amazingly, all the graphics on this Lighthouse Cleanser push were done with a stencil. It becomes obvious why the decal method was superior, as the detailing on this image could not be precise enough to compete with those found by using a decal. It wound up giving the cleanser can a somewhat cartoonish look with inconsistencies that would never be found by using a decal. However, this is what Armour and Company wanted and the end result was still a magnificent contribution to early American advertising. It measures 7.5" x 4.5" and dates to 1915. *Courtesy of Dick Marrah.* **$1,000**

Unusual in design, Yeast Foam produced this 7" x 2" advertisement sometime around 1910. *Courtesy of Dick and Diane Kinsey.* **$400**

This two-color door push dates from 1910 and measures 7" x 3.5". *Courtesy of Dick and Diane Kinsey.* **$600**

A beautiful addition to any door push collection would be this graphic Clark Flour advertisement. It measures 8.5" x 4" and appears to date from around 1920. *Courtesy of Dick and Diane Kinsey.* **$875**

Dr. Pepper had this die-cut door push produced in the 1930s. Several other manufacturers had similar die-cut ones produced as well, including Coca-Cola. This example measures 4" x 26" overall and has its familiar 10, 2, and 4 logo at each side.
Courtesy of Rick and Pamela Stevens. $1,850

Here's a close-up of the manufacturer's stamping on the Dr. Pepper door push, complete with manufacturer's name, city, state, and its United States patent number.
Courtesy of Rick and Pamela Stevens.

Hires Root Beer was a huge success all the way back to the earlier part of the twentieth century. This advertisement is a full-span door push that I believe dates to the 1950s. It measures 2.5" x 31".
Courtesy of Bob Newman. $350

will not affect your throat

This rare Pippins Cigar match striker dates from around 1910. Their famous logo featuring a large red apple has been found on a variety of other porcelain advertisements as well. This one measures 6" x 4".
Courtesy of Dick and Diane Kinsey. $825

Some say that black cats can bring bad luck, but ominously that was the trademark for Craven "A" Virginia Cigarettes. Such an appropriate graphic does not seem to coincide with the touting of "will not affect your throat" on this 13" x 3.5" sign dating from the 1920s. A close examination of the cigarette box reveals that its contents make up a ten pack, half the size of today's industry standard.
Courtesy of Bob Newman. $600

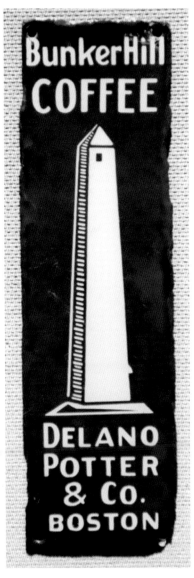

Vicks produced many styles of door pushes through the years. This newer version, dating from sometime around the 1930s, is scarce. It measures 7" x 4.5".
Courtesy of Dick and Diane Kinsey. $450

Queen Shears was one of the lesser-known cutlery manufacturers in America. This early 1920s advertisement measures 9" x 4".
Author's collection. $700

Most likely used as a door push, this Bunker Hill Coffee sign measures 10" x 3". Although it has only two colors, the large central graphic of an obelisk adds considerable appeal. It dates from the 1920s.
Courtesy of John Bobroff. $750

This oval advertisement from the Automobile Owners Association of America measures 3.25" x 5" and dates from the 1920s. Were four grommet holes really necessary? Considering its size, probably not.
Courtesy of Bob Newman. $250

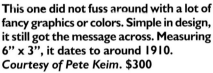

This one did not fuss around with a lot of fancy graphics or colors. Simple in design, it still got the message across. Measuring 6" x 3", it dates to around 1910. *Courtesy of Pete Keim.* $300

This license plate attachment dates from the 1920s. Automobile theft was already becoming a serious problem in America as the bottom part of this tag will attest. It talks of a $100 reward being offered for the arrest of any person stealing this automobile. It measures 4" x 3". *Courtesy of Sue Gladden.* $100

This die-cut hexagonal license tag was produced for the California State Employees Association in the 1930s. It measures approximately 3.5" square without the mounting tab. *Courtesy of Jeff Kaye.* $250

Here's a license plate attachment that was designated to show that this vehicle's owner was a member of the Shelburne Falls, Massachusetts, Fire Department. It measures 4.5" square, not including its mounting tab. *Courtesy of John Bobroff.* $300

This American Automobile Association oval tag from the Oregon State Motor Association measures 3" x 4" and dates to the 1930s.
Courtesy of Mick Hoover. $200

Looking at the complexity of this Union Automobile Club cloisonné tag, it appears that it was an expensive proposition to manufacture. It was produced by the H. R. Hudson Company of Los Angeles in the 1930s and measures 3.5" x 6".
Courtesy of Dennis Griffin. $300

Another highly detailed tag is this die-cut Republic Auto Insurance Company of Detroit example. A close examination will reveal the lack of porcelain in the cloisonné separation under the eagle's wings. This was intentional, probably to help separate the colors and give additional relief to the eagle's wings. It measures 3.5" x 5" and dates from the 1920s.
Courtesy of Bob Newman. $250

This beautiful vertical oval tag dates from the 1920s. The unusual-looking device as its central image is not an old gas pump, but rather an intersection warning pillar with illuminated top sign. These were common in many of the larger cities prior to the modern traffic lights we have today. It measures 4.5" x 3". *Courtesy of Bob Newman.* $300

This red, white, and blue die-cut shield tag was produced for the National Automobile Association most likely around 1930.
Courtesy of Mick Hoover. $200

Still another pair of quality advertising is featured here. The smaller sign measures 3" x 10", its use most likely limited as a point of purchase advertisement or a door push. The larger sign measures 3" x 24" and could be used not only as a point of purchase advertisement if the need arose, but could also function as a door push or door kick plate as well. They both date to around 1920.
Courtesy of Pete Keim. $350 each

It is a shame this 3" Anthracite Motor Club tag is not in better condition. However, its outstanding graphics and rarity warrants inclusion here. The center image of the miner wearing the antiquated torch helmet makes this piece a standout. It dates from the 1920s. *Courtesy of John Bobroff.* $250

The exact origin of this REO tag is uncertain. It measures approximately 3" overall and appears to date from the 1920s. I would suspect it was placed on the radiator grill at the front of one of their beautiful cars.
Courtesy of Bob Newman. $200

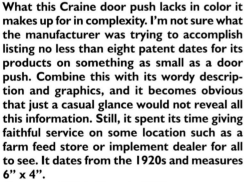

What this Craine door push lacks in color it makes up for in complexity. I'm not sure what the manufacturer was trying to accomplish listing no less than eight patent dates for its products on something as small as a door push. Combine this with its wordy description and graphics, and it becomes obvious that just a casual glance would not reveal all this information. Still, it spent its time giving faithful service on some location such as a farm feed store or implement dealer for all to see. It dates from the 1920s and measures 6" x 4".
Courtesy of Dick Marrah. $400

Both Pennsylvania and Indiana are listed on this State Automobile Association Insurance tag dating from the 1920s.
Courtesy of Sue Gladden. $150

Not quite a shield design, but die-cut to a similar configuration, is this American States tag dating to around 1930. It measures 4" square.
Courtesy of Bob Newman. $300

This gorgeous 3.5" diameter Sioux City Auto Club tag appears to date from the 1920s. Its graphic Sioux Indian chief as its central image gives this advertisement plenty of eye appeal.
Courtesy of Bob Newman. $400

In later years oval door pushes seem to have become the predominant design. Orange Crush is featured on this example dating from around 1940. It measures 9.5" x 4".
Courtesy of Bob Newman. $800

Chapter Eight:
A Porcelain Potpourri

Porcelain enamel advertising has come to mean substantially more than just signs. The list of items produced through the years could fill a book in itself. Ashtrays, dispensers, promotional advertisements, neon's, bicycle racks, hat badges, park benches, sidewalk signs, countertop displays, vending machines, and dozens of other products were manufactured with the common factor of having a porcelain message.

Through the years, many dispensers were manufactured with a combination of stainless steel and porcelain enamel. Porcelain's unique ability to advertise coupled with its easy cleanup made it an optimal choice for the manufacturer and end user as well. Seen here is a rare small-sized Orange Crush dispenser dating from the 1930s. It measures 20" x 16".
Courtesy of Dick and Diane Kinsey. $2,000

Porcelain enamel advertising production was not in full swing until after the year 1900 in America. Up until this point, advertisers still needed to rely heavily on the production capabilities of such countries as England and Germany, who were already well versed in the art. This beautiful multi-colored sample piece was produced by a German company for distribution at the Chicago World Fair in 1893. It measures 6.5" x 4".
Courtesy of Pete Keim. $400

Most manufacturers produced salesmen sample giveaways. Ingram-Richardson was no exception. This multi-color ashtray dating from the 1920s advertises their ability to produce porcelain enamel signs. It measures approximately 5" in diameter. *Courtesy of Dennis and Jeanne Weber*. $225

It appears that this 6" x 8" porcelain enamel tray was intended to be used at a pharmacy to help sort compounds or medications. It dates from around the 1920s or 1930s. *Courtesy of Mick Hoover*. $200

Here's an example of a larger-sized advertisement that was designated for exterior use with neon. Although the neon has been totally removed, the frame and advertising itself are still intact and in excellent condition. This is a three-dimensional piece that measures approximately 62" x 72" and is 10" thick. Notice that the majority of the circular Westinghouse logo was actually manufactured separately from the body of the sign and would attach to its top when assembled. It dates from the 1930s. *Courtesy of Mick Hoover*. $1,250

The heyday of Western Union saw the employment of thousands of young men whose purpose was to quickly deliver and receive messages in the city. Many of these messengers were provided a company bicycle to get them around to their various pick up and drop off points efficiently. This Western Union advertisement is affixed to a bicycle rack that some of the larger offices needed to keep their bicycles corralled. As you may have guessed, the sign is two-sided. It measures 32" x 48" and dates from the 1920s.
Courtesy of Mick Hoover. $1,050

Here is a close up of a very old porcelain enamel hat badge. Western Union and American District Telegraph had an operational agreement and although they were competitors, can be found listed together on many early advertisements. The "101" seen at the bottom center is the employee identification number. It measures approximately 1.5" x 4".
Private collection. $250

Mutual Telephone Company was one of thousands of independents across the United States that operated prior to the 1960s. This die-cut red, white, and blue shield sign was designed to be mounted on a coin-operated pay station. The hole in the center was for the transmitter. Unfortunately, somewhere in its past this beautiful advertisement was separated from its original telephone box. It measures 9.5" x 8" and dates from around the 1920s.
Courtesy of Mick Hoover. $825

One of the most unusual applications of porcelain enamel advertising has to be this park bench that was manufactured for Union Service Stations. Apparently, it was designed to be used in the waiting room of a lubrication shop. Although it's difficult to tell in the photograph, the bench's seat is wood grain and is also made of porcelain enamel. Very unique indeed! It dates to around 1930.
Courtesy of Dennis Griffin. $4,000

Here is a rare neon advertisement for Rainbow Gasoline. It dates from the 1930s and measures approximately 3" x 6".
Courtesy of Mike Mihkelson.
$5,750

Shell produced hundreds of die-cut clamshell porcelain signs for their roadside station advertisements throughout the years. Few, however, were ever manufactured with a neon border around their perimeter. This one dates from the 1940s and measures approximately 45" square.
Courtesy of Mike Mihkelson.
$2,500

The Canadian manufacturer C.C.M. had this Joycycle countertop advertisement produced in the 1920s. It depicts a child in a sailor suit happily riding their Joycycle. It measures 6" x 13" and is one-sided.
Courtesy of Jeff Kaye. $2,000

A double-sided standup sidewalk advertisement for Bristol Laundry. Measuring 30" x 16", it dates from the 1930s. *Courtesy of Sue Gladden.* $500

Most petroleum companies also did a huge business in the motor oil market. This 23" square case was designed to hold tall-style quart oil bottles. As you can see, the case started off being a Mobiloil dispenser; however, at some point it was partially transformed to sell Standard Red Crown Motor Oil as well. It dates from the 1920s. *Courtesy of Mick Hoover.* $1,100

At first glance it may not be apparent that this is a door from a Round Oak Stove. Most of the earlier stove manufacturers used porcelain to some degree on their products. Round Oak placed its logo front and center on at least one of its oven doors. Although the stove seems to have gone by the wayside, the door still serves as a historic reminder of its lineage. It measures 10" x 17" and dates to the 1920s. *Courtesy of John Bobroff.* $200

I felt a close up of the Round Oak Stove advertisement was in order. The Indian chief Dowagiac with headband makes their logo a desirable part of an advertising collection. Round Oak manufactured hundreds of assorted advertisements through the years, which helped put them in a position as a large manufacturer of that era. *Courtesy of John Bobroff.*

A spectacular sidewalk advertisement for Hercules Gasoline. For petrol collectors, this is the type of thing dreams are made of. It appears to be from the 1920s and measures 48" x 30". *Courtesy of Dennis Griffin.* **$4,500**

Most of the larger petroleum companies used specific designs for their service stations. This architectural standardization was believed to make better identity with the customer and was the consumer's assurance of the same quality products and services no matter where they were purchased. The Mobil Corporation incorporated into one of its standard building designs the use of a cupola with a die-cut weathervane promoting their famous Pegasus trademark. Although it came complete with a set of directionals, everything was welded into place and was not actually functional. One of these scarce directional sets is seen here. It measures approximately 40" tall and 25" wide overall. These date from the 1930s and 1940s.
Author's collection. $1,400

Many petroleum companies launched major campaigns to promote clean restrooms to the motoring public. They knew this would be in their best interest, as it was a method to lure customers in, therefore producing higher sales. The Mobil Corporation produced this die-cut sign, affixed to a paper towel dispenser, that let patrons know that the station management was doing everything possible to provide clean restroom conditions for all. It is unusual to see one of these signs still mounted to its original dispenser, which measures 16" x 11". It dates from the 1940s.
Courtesy of Rod Krupka. $550

Many of us have run across the Steamro Red Hots porcelain strip sign. Few of us, however, have ever actually seen the machine that these came off of, so I thought it would be good to give you an idea as to its application. This machine was built in the 1930s and had a porcelain sign affixed to each side. Just one more way the advertising world utilized porcelain.
Author's collection. $750

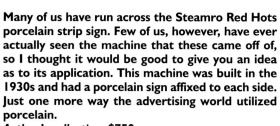

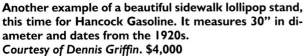

Another example of a beautiful sidewalk lollipop stand, this time for Hancock Gasoline. It measures 30" in diameter and dates from the 1920s.
Courtesy of Dennis Griffin. $4,000

This National District Telegraph Company call box was used to summon a messenger in the late 1800s. It's among the rarest of the "tombstone" designs, and utilizes a seldom-found message-sent window, giving the user a clear indication that their message was transmitted.
Author's collection. $2,000

The nine round disks shown here are actually color samples produced by American Porcelain. Each measures approximately 3" in diameter and I believe them to date from the 1940s or 1950s. As can be seen on the samples, each one is individually numbered and goes as high as number 237.
Private collection. $30 each

Like many of the advertisements produced in the early 1940s, this serving tray has a patriotic motif. Although its use was generic, it is ink stamped on the reverse, "Baltimore Enamel Maryland." It measures 13" in diameter. *Courtesy of Jeff Kaye.* $300

Here is a 5.5" diameter ashtray for Hardwick Speedi-Baker ranges. The style of the product advertised would lead one to believe that this ashtray dates from the 1930s. *Courtesy of Bob Newman.* $150

It appears this 5" diameter Reddy Kilowatt porcelain advertisement was used as an ashtray. It dates from the 1950s. *Courtesy of Bob Newman.* $100

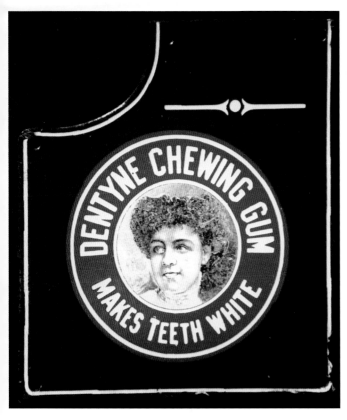

This die-cut advertisement is actually a side panel from an early chewing gum dispenser. The handsome looking woman shown in the advertisement is supposed to be demonstrating how Dentyne made her teeth white. Scary! It measures approximately 10" x 9" and dates from around 1910. *Courtesy of John Bobroff.* $700

Expositions were commonly held in the late 1800s and early 1900s. They were somewhat similar to our modern-day state fairs insofar as they displayed the latest technology of the period. This souvenir from an unknown exposition in the year 1900 comes in the form of a serving tray that measures 12" in diameter. It is unlikely that this was given away, but more likely sold at a nominal cost to those eagerly seeking a souvenir from the Exposition. One thing's for sure: it was manufactured by the best place in town, Baltimore Enamel and Novelty Company, and is ink stamped and fired onto its reverse side as such. *Author's collection.* $450

This rare Good Humor ice cream box dates from the 1920s. It could be conveniently carried by a vendor to such places as ball games and other places where the public could easily spot what tasty treat was being dispensed. Measuring 12" x 18" x 10", its wonderful early Good Humor advertisement is on two sides. *Courtesy of Jeff Kaye.* $3,000

This is a Telegraph Company messenger bicycle rack. This is an early one, as indicated by the lettering font and pointing hand. The sign is ink stamped "Ingram-Richardson Beaver Falls Pennsylvania," and "100 Williams Street New York." Measuring 18" x 30", it dates from around 1900. *Courtesy of Mick Hoover.* $2,000

Here's another example of an item that was most likely given away to distributors. This Cherry Blossom Boot Polish shoe stand was designed for the customer to be either sitting or standing and have their shoes shined up to perfection. Obviously, Cherry Blossom wanted to maximize their exposure as it would be almost impossible to make their logo any larger on this 17" square shoe stand. I believe it to be quite early, dating from around 1915. *Courtesy of Jeff Kaye.* $2,200

A gorgeous standup lollipop sidewalk advertisement for Richfield Ethyl Gasoline. The sign itself measures 26" in diameter. Notice the small proprietary sign affixed to the stand. It dates from the 1920s. *Courtesy of Dennis Griffin.* $3,500

A rare sidewalk lollipop stand for Zerolene. Notice the unusual multifaceted iron base. It measures approximately 53" tall x 19" wide and dates from the 1920s. *Courtesy of Dennis Griffin.* $2,750

Most sidewalk lollipop stands utilized a 30" diameter advertisement. This one is somewhat unusual as its diameter is only 19.5". It dates from the late 1920s. *Courtesy of Dennis Griffin.* $2,500

One of the rarest of all call boxes is featured on this District Telegraph and Telephone unit that dates from the late 1800s. These boxes were normally designed to send a coded telegraph message from station to station summoning a messenger. This one, however, is very unusual insofar as it is actually a telephone as well, as can be seen by the outside terminal receiver and transmitter. It measures approximately 15" x 8" overall. *Author's collection.* $2,300

This trio of disease has been photographed to show you one of the more unusual albeit unsanitary uses for porcelain enamel. These were all used by railroads and are, from left to right, Rock Island Lines, Burlington Route, and Central of Georgia. It was common to find these in stations, on platforms, and even in parlor cars being used in place of an open window to rid oneself of finished chewing tobacco, which was a common practice up until 1920. These pieces all measure approximately 10" each.
Courtesy of John Bobroff. $200 each

Here's a small-sized 13" x 8" countertop sign advertising Herman's Salads. Although they tout their "Famous" Dutch salads, they appear to be only a local company that was located on Geary Boulevard in San Francisco, California. *Author's collection.* $500

I believe the origin of this Rohde's LaFayette Hall Cigar advertisement was to be placed on a countertop cigar display. Its small 1.5" x 7" dimension would indicate that it needed to be in close proximity to the customer and a countertop would be ideal placement. Whatever the case it's apparently early, dating from around 1910, and shows the ever-popular five-cent price for their product.
Courtesy of Bob Newman. $450

As a promotional item, Tennessee Enamel Manufacturing Company of Nashville produced this line-drawing style image of The Hermitage in Cumberland Valley around the 1930s. It measures approximately 20" x 26" and was manufactured to appear matted. Andrew Jackson would have been proud.
Author's collection. $700

A close-up of the central image area reveals the detail work and artistry that was created to produce this sign.
Author's collection.

The original manufacturer's label is still affixed to the back side of The Hermitage sign. I could not resist letting you see for yourself its story.
Author's collection.

THE HERMITAGE

The Hermitage, famous old home of President Andrew Jackson, is nestled in the heart of the Cumberland Valley near Nashville, Tennessee. It was built by Jackson and his wife Rachel in 1819 upon his return from the Seminole Wars. Here Jackson spent the last 25 years of his life. The original "Hermitage" burned to the ground in 1834 but was immediately re-built on its old foundation. In 1856 it was sold to the State of Tennessee by Jackson's adopted son. Since that time its sun-drenched gardens with its pebbled paths, its old-fashioned flowers and beautiful magnolia trees, have delighted thousands of visitors yearly from all parts of the world. The house itself, complete with the original furnishings and personal property of Jackson, is one of the most charming old plantation homesteads in the entire Southland. In a quiet corner of the beautiful garden adjoining the house, rest "Old Hickory" and his beloved wife.

"The Hermitage" is truly a national shrine.

This reproduction was made by fusing glass onto steel at a temperature of 1600 degrees and will last forever.

—Tennessee Enamel Mfg. Co., Nashville, Tenn.

Chapter Nine:
Parting Shots

Many of you may find this final chapter to be the most interesting. It focuses primarily on the porcelain enamel advertising acquired by some of the fine people I have met in my travels. Their beautiful collections are a source of pride and historical significance. Each one of the pieces that they have secured represents a part of their life and has its own silent story to tell. These people are true historians, as they are preserving for future generations that which was never considered a collectible artifact when it was manufactured.

Also, this chapter features some of the few remaining porcelain enamel advertisements that can be seen adorning miscellaneous buildings throughout America. Scenes like these are getting few and far between and truly represent an image of our American advertising heritage. Enjoy the tour!

A vast assortment of eye-appealing goodies awaits visitors to the garage of Terry and Dawn Hubert of Brighton, Michigan. A keen interest in the hobby along with their generous nature make this garage a place for a warm welcome to collectors. Terry, aka Cheeseman, has also a local reputation for hosting a fine petroleum collectibles show featuring many porcelain signs every year. Visit him on the Internet at www.bigcheesepetro.com. *Courtesy of Terry and Dawn Hubert.*

This large-scale porcelain and neon advertisement was part of the downtown scene in Woodland, California. As you can see by its size relative to the rest of the structure, it could easily be seen from a distance. Although the large building marquee will most likely never wind up as a collector's item, the smaller "Drugs" sign protruding from the side of the building and its cute mortar and pestle hanging below would probably be keepers. This advertisement most likely dates to the 1930s and is a testimonial to porcelain advertising's longevity as it is still giving faithful service to Corner Drug Company to this day.

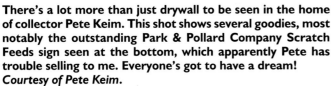

There's a lot more than just drywall to be seen in the home of collector Pete Keim. This shot shows several goodies, most notably the outstanding Park & Pollard Company Scratch Feeds sign seen at the bottom, which apparently Pete has trouble selling to me. Everyone's got to have a dream!
Courtesy of Pete Keim.

In this section of his beautiful home, Pete has sorted out some of the more generic items as well as some beautiful blue and white door pushes. Notice the outstanding Ingram-Richardson advertisement at center.
Courtesy of Pete Keim.

If door pushes are your thing, check out this nifty collection at countertop level in the home of Pete Keim.
Courtesy of Pete Keim.

Another wall shot showing the varied subject matter and high quality of Pete Keim's collection. *Courtesy of Pete Keim.*

A corner wall shot gives an indication as to the serious nature of this collection. These outstanding items, most notably the door pushes, are a collection in themselves and have found a wonderful home at the residence of Pete Keim. *Courtesy of Pete Keim.*

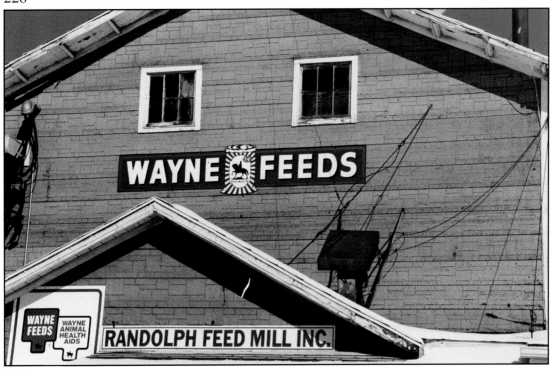

A winter drive through the countryside turned up this remnant from earlier days in Randolph, Wisconsin. The large Wayne Feeds sign measures approximately 12' wide and was done as one solid stamping.

My back road traveling has offered me the experience of seeing many out-of-the-way advertisements still in use today. Normally I love to tell people about these adventures and the resulting finds they have produced. But there seems to be a high degree of these wayside artifacts that come up missing, especially after being published in one of my previous books. So, unfortunately, I am not going to give you readers the exact whereabouts of a couple of the more rare and high-dollar items that I have found in my travels. The Authorized Cessna Service neon and porcelain advertisement seen here is one such example. Its desirability combined with its rarity and high collector value make it one of the last remaining treasures still intact and giving faithful service at a local airport. For those of you still insisting to know the location of this gem, I will give you a clue: It is in the United States. Good luck!

Here's an innovative approach to privacy while satisfying your collecting desire. Darryl Fritsch has literally plastered his fence with the stuff he loves — porcelain enamel advertising! *Courtesy of Darryl Fritsch.*

For all the thousands of Coca-Cola buttons that were produced through the years, one would think that many of these would still be in service, especially considering their logo has not changed. However, this is not the case, as you could drive for days without finding an original advertisement still intact. The pair that has been captured here is on a still-operating drugstore complete with soda fountain in Ashton, Idaho.

This die-cut Frontier Station sign was spotted a short distance from one of America's most popular antiquing areas, Snohomish, Washington.

Here's another example of a high-dollar advertisement still in its original setting perched high on a mountainside. Again, as with the Cessna sign, I would just as soon not tell you its exact location, but it should be obvious by the appearance of the landscape that it is somewhere out west. If you are thinking about scoring this one, you better have a fairly good set of grappling rope and hooks in addition to a nice life insurance policy, as anything but the most careful of removals might result in death.

A closer look at this rock-mounted beauty will bring attention to some of its history. It will also show how precarious any removal attempt may be. It was originally a 6' Wasatch Petroleum sign that at some point in its history was painted over with the Phillips 66 logo—which has been almost totally removed through time and weathering. A careful study can reveal the Phillips 66 logo. I hope this historic artifact will stay there for years as a reminder of days gone by.

The ghost town of Arnold, Michigan, turned up this dilapidated general store. As if still beckoning customers, a porcelain IGA sign stands ready to bring in the crowds.

Gas Pump Ronnie of Hesperia, California, has created a historic assemblage of petroleum-related artifacts. All of this is themed around his well-known Black Cat Garage, complete with gas pumps and an attendant's booth. A closer review of items will reveal the two California Automobile Club diamond-shaped directional signs hanging above the garage door as well as many other goodies.

A silent reminder of a better time still stands near Jennings, Kansas.
These Standard signs were made in the thousands, but are rarely seen
today. Long gone is its glass globe in the shape of a flame perched above
the sign's oval framework.

Although somewhat isolated at their location, the display room and workshop of Mick and Christine Hoover
of Mackay, Idaho, show them being anything but isolated from the collector's world. I have known Mick
and Christine for years and have been to their house many times in Idaho and always marvel at their ability to turn up new finds. Like myself, Mick and Christine take an avid interest in many collectibles aside
from porcelain advertising and even when it comes to porcelain, their interest is diversified among not
only petroleum but country store and other subject matters as well.
Courtesy of Mick Hoover.

A corner shot of Mick and Christine's garage reveals that there is little left-over space on the walls or floor. The large Westinghouse Appliance marquee has been pictured in previous pages of this book. I am glad they found an appropriate way to display this historic artifact.
Courtesy of Mick Hoover.

California Highway 16 is the main street in Woodland, California. Much to my surprise, these two porcelain neon advertisements were still giving service on a dealership downtown. We had all better enjoy these few remaining artifacts while we can, as this type of thing is almost extinct.

My drive through Woodland, California, also turned up this Federal Burglar Alarm porcelain sign still mounted on its original box.

America's famous Route 66 traversed between Chicago and Los Angeles and went through the heartland of America. Near Peach Springs, Arizona, this Texaco roadside sign serves as a reminder of those earlier times when this route was the 'expressway' to the west.

Within the Black Hills of South Dakota are situated the towns of Deadwood and Sturgis. Not quite as well known to tourists, but just to the north is the old mining town of Spearfish. Its main street is an assemblage of restaurants, taverns, and retail shops, one of which sports an original die-cut Budweiser advertisement from the 1930s. Although Spearfish does a nominal tourist business during the summer months, the town literally comes alive during the annual Sturgis Motorcycle Rally.

In the California desert at a place the locals call Four Corners, Kramer Antiques and Pottery has this large set of outbuildings adjoining their store. As you can see, there is a nice assortment of porcelain advertising as well as some older gas station memorabilia on the property.

This view shows the antique shop as well as another outbuilding at the Four Corners location. One thing's for sure: they've got the only show in town. Actually, they've got the only show for a hundred miles in any direction. It's a great place to stop to rid yourself of that antiquing urge.

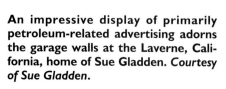

An impressive display of primarily petroleum-related advertising adorns the garage walls at the Laverne, California, home of Sue Gladden. *Courtesy of Sue Gladden.*

Although it is not unusual for many collectors to turn their garage space into a display room of advertising, what is unusual is the quality of the items that are seen in these photographs. Dennis Griffin of Orange, California has assembled a vast and impressive array of early petroleum-related advertising. An assortment of neon porcelain advertising and petroleum-related smalls are on display in these views. *Courtesy of Dennis Griffin.*

The old and the new have come together in this remodeled Dairy Queen located in St. Joseph, Missouri. Although a considerable amount of money has been spent updating this structure, most notably the new roof and plastic light-up street sign in the background, they elected to leave the original neon and porcelain advertisement intact. A wise move, indeed.

As most everyone knows, there are very few porcelain advertisements still doing service that were originally installed in the 1930s or 1940s. This winter scene shows a porcelain with neon Rexall sign doing its duty in Panguitch, Utah. Similar Rexall signs were installed by the thousands across America. Many are still intact today as painted-over remnants of yesteryear.

Ray's Barber Shop in Flagstaff, Arizona, probably has the last remaining porcelain that could be up for grabs in town. Ray doesn't seem too concerned, however, as he can be seen through the center window reading the morning paper. These barber shop signs are just about the last vestiges of our porcelain era still remaining intact.

Dick Marrah of Penryn, California, has put his collecting interests in high gear for many years. The walls of his beautiful home in the foothills of the Sierra Nevada Mountains reflect his never-ending pursuit to acquire these historical artifacts. Although Dick specializes in bus line advertising, you can see he's not scared to go for the other good stuff out there as well.
Courtesy of Dick Marrah.

Another wall shot inside the home of Dick Marrah. Some of these bus signs are mind blowing, such as the Peerless Stages sign at the left. I have only one question for you, Dick. Where do you keep finding this stuff?
Courtesy of Dick Marrah.

I was speechless upon entering the home of well-known collectors Dick and Diane Kinsey of Modesto, California. Their museum-quality collection is the result of years of time and thousands of miles of travel. I'll start you off with a side shot of their parlor room, which has a country store flavor. Although this particular section of the home has few porcelain advertisements, I could not help but show you the wonderful assortment of historical artifacts on display.
Courtesy of Dick and Diane Kinsey.

Looking the opposite direction in this panorama is another eye full. Spend some time and look at all this marvelous stuff. All of these things are extremely difficult to acquire and have been carefully selected by Dick and Diane for their uniqueness and character. Absolutely amazing.
Courtesy of Dick and Diane Kinsey.

A shot from one corner of the kitchen reveals some outstanding porcelain enamel door pushes, a Fry's Pure Cocoa display stand with assorted western-themed plates, and a highly-desirable Heinz Pickle string holder.
Courtesy of Dick and Diane Kinsey.

The bathroom, of all places, is where I was able to get this shot. Keeping the theme of such a location are porcelain enamel advertisements of a sanitary or medicinal nature. Most collectors would never find it necessary to take a book to the bathroom, as their mind would be more than occupied with what's on the walls.
Courtesy of Dick and Diane Kinsey.

A hallway shot reveals more interesting items in the home of Dick and Diane Kinsey.
Courtesy of Dick and Diane Kinsey.

An automobile accident was almost the end result of my driving past this storefront on the Pacific Coast Highway in Long Beach, California. What collector wouldn't be enticed by the selection of porcelain enamel advertising displayed in the front window, which beckons you to come inside to view the real jackpot. It seems to be a common practice in antique malls to put out a few bait items in the storefront windows that, upon inquiry, will be met with comments such as "Oh, that's not for sale." No such fear here, however, as everything seen in the photograph and all the rest inside is up for grabs at the Long Beach Antique and Collectible Mall.

An interior shot. Porcelain and tin signs, advertising clocks, thermometers, figurals; you name it, they've got it all.

No, this is not a dream or a staged photograph. This is actually an interior shot of an aisle way inside the Long Beach Antique and Collectible Mall. It's like a kid in a candy store for me.

In the mountains of the American Southwest is one of the most unusual towns I've ever seen: Oatman, Arizona. Its claim to fame appears to be its many wild burros that have taken residence in and around the main street of town. These animals are the descendents of those brought in during the mining rush in the late 1800s, which were subsequently set free as the mining disappeared in later years. Today, they are totally tame and are most appreciative of handouts from tourists. In an alley off the main street I spotted this Flamo Gas-Equipped Cabins porcelain sign on the side of a building. Not wanting to miss an opportunity for a photograph, I've captured not only the porcelain advertisement but a picture of Heidi Abbott making this burro's day with a handful of nuts. As most of us collectors would be interested in the porcelain sign, it appears the burro is only interested in what is going in its mouth.

Many cities across America, especially those in rural locations, had civic clubs for the younger folks such as the FFA and 4H. This 4H sign has seen better days, being used at some point for target practice. It is still giving service to the community of West Liberty, Ohio.

Another prominent collector located in California is Mike Mihkelson of Long Beach. Any true collector of petroleum advertising would feel quite at home in his living room, as evidenced by the assortment of goodies on the walls. *Courtesy of Mike Mihkelson.*

Here's a different interior view of Mike Mihkelson's display. I have been in many collectors' homes and seen plenty through the years, and I can tell you this tasteful array will keep you looking all day long. Notice the rare Seaside Gasoline porcelain and neon station sign on the back wall. *Courtesy of Mike Mihkelson.*

246

Harley's Garage has been a desert oasis for motorists since 1946. Here's one of the few remaining original United Service advertisements still intact. It is located on the main street in Mesquite, Nevada. Keep your moving van at home though, as Tammy Leavitt, the manager who has been there more than thirty years, says she's had many opportunities to sell this piece to eager collectors. For now, it is going to stay where Harley wanted it: high and dry in the desert air. I'm not sure about the oval Ford advertisement seen to its left, as it is obviously painted and is no doubt different from its original advertising.

Pam and Jon Pomeroy of Covina, California, have found a wonderful way to mix business with pleasure. Here are two shots of their vast display area showing many of their collecting interests, which is located in their business shop. A walk-through would give one the illusion of being in advertising wonderland, as it seems to never end and a new discovery awaits the eye every moment. As you can see by the height of the ceiling, this is not a small display area. This is what collecting is about and why collectors will do most anything to preserve and display these artifacts appropriately. *Courtesy of Pam and Jon Pomeroy.*

One of the benchmarks of a true collector is their ability to cram as much great stuff into a display area as possible. Mission accomplished in the home of Rick and Pamela Stevens of Wyandotte, Michigan. Their beautiful assemblage of early Americana tastefully adorns most every room in the house. This wide angle shot shows how the television plays a minor role in the overall scheme of things in the living room.
Courtesy of Rick and Pamela Stevens.

Switching to the dining room area, again we find a wonderful assortment of early Americana. Notice the porcelain-coated electric barber pole. At its top is a rare original globe, which was found in an antique shop mistakenly identified as a glass basketball lampshade.
Courtesy of Rick and Pamela Stevens.

Moving to the upstairs a vacant bedroom serves as another display area, this time with the focus on Coca-Cola.
Courtesy of Rick and Pamela Stevens.

Through the years I have repeatedly visited the mountain home of John Bobroff and I'm always fascinated by the ready assortment of porcelain advertising that is displayed. I have photographed in his home for my previous books, but I felt the active nature of his display warrants a second look. Here is a shot in his entranceway hall. If you compare this to the photograph I took over ten years ago at the same location, you can see how his wall has changed. As a side note, I might add that my most recent visit to his house passed by burned out homes, charred automobiles, and forest area that was only two blocks from his house. Fortunately the fire was controlled at that point and John's historical collection had been saved. A happy ending for John and the collecting world alike!

It's no secret to many of you that John is a retired California State Highway Patrolman. His interest in police memorabilia is seen in this view of the wall area at the top of his stairway.

Reflecting his long-time interest in railroad memorabilia, this shot shows John's railroad room on the upper level. Like the rest of his house, it is crammed full of porcelain advertisements that were collected over a period of decades.

There has been a rumor going around that I really don't collect this stuff, I just like to write books. Well, yes, I like writing books, but I do collect these artifacts and it has been a huge part of my interests for most of my life. In my previous books, I decided to leave out pictures taken in my home in favor of some of our hobby's most respected and devoted collectors, but I am proud of my collecting efforts too, and I thought you would enjoy me sharing this important part of my life with you. We'll start off with a long shot of the bar room. As you can see by the wall, my interest is not limited to porcelain signs alone, but to other interesting items such as advertising clocks. *Author's collection.*

A straight-ahead shot from my position in the bar room reveals a set of light-up Jennings slot machines of different denominations and from assorted casinos in the Reno, Nevada, area. Above those is a tasty selection of porcelain advertising, most notably the Rand McNally Hotel die-cut arrowhead, one of the most sought-after of all country store advertisements. *Author's collection.*

Facing my viewfinder the other direction can be seen, along the same wall, a 1920s roulette table. *Author's collection.*

Going to the lower level produces an image of shelves loaded with miscellaneous tasty goodies. I've collected a variety of things throughout my life, and I believe Thomas Edison must be my patron saint as I have a particular affection for things that are operated by electricity, such as globes, motion displays, and other light-up devices. *Author's collection.*

Another shot in the same room reveals a different selection of items, again with many of them using electricity in one way or another. *Author's collection.*

Still another view in the same room reveals a continuation of the shelving along with some floor display space. Not to be ignored is the blow fish hanging from the ceiling. *Author's collection.*

A curved wall area is the perfect place to display curved signs.
Author's collection.

A shot in the corner of the kitchen shows a display cabinet full of porcelain enamel telegraph call boxes.
Author's collection.

Here's a shot looking back in the corner of the great room. Although there seems to be a copious amount of items to catch one's eye, most collectors of porcelain enamel advertising would probably focus on the Kelly Tires sign at upper right. I hope you've enjoyed the little tour and I look forward to visiting other collectors in future years.
Author's collection.

Manufacturers

A list of the manufacturers' names that can be found on the signs in this book appears at the end of this chapter. Most of the major companies will be present as they produced high quantities of signs. Street addresses are not listed because some companies did business at more than one location.

Many of the companies were manufacturers of very different products, such as stove castings, building panels, kitchenware, and other utilitarian items. Although it is difficult to establish, the dates listed will give you an idea as to a particular company's "heyday." A (*) designates that limited information is available for the years of production.

It is interesting to note that one of the most frequently encountered names found on signs, F. M. BURDICK, of Chicago, was a distributor, not a manufacturer. This will be true of a few of the other companies as well.

ACTON BURROWS CO., TORONTO, CANADA, 1900-1920
AMERICAN SIGN COMPANY, 1920-1930
AMERICAN VALVE & ENAMELING CORP., 1928-1970
BALTIMORE ENAMEL, BALTIMORE, MD, 1897-1943
BEACH, COSHOCTON, OHIO, 1910-1940
BEATTY MCMILLAN CO., DETROIT, MICHIGAN*
BELLAIRE STAMPING (B.S.), CHICAGO, ILLINOIS
BILLY NEWTON COMPANY, MINNESOTA, 1930-1940
BOB WHITE SIGN CO., MILWAUKEE, WISCONSIN
BRILLIANT MANUFACTURING CO., PHILADELPHIA, PENN-
    SYLVANIA, 1910-1930
BURDICK, CHICAGO, ILLINOIS, 1895-1950
C. ROBERT DOLD, OFFENBURG, GERMANY, 1905-1920
CALIFORNIA METAL ENAMELING COMPANY (CAMEO),
    LOS ANGELES, CALIFORNIA
CAMEO GILA, 1904-1980
CHICAGO VITREOUS ENAMEL PRODUCT COMPANY,
    1930-1980
CRICHTON CURL ENAMEL CO., ELLWOOD CITY, PA,
    1905-1920
ENAMELED IRON CO., BEAVER FALLS, PA, 1892-1900
F. FRANCIS AND SONS LTD., LONGON*
F. E. MARSLAND, NY HARTMAN (STEEL CO. OF ELLWOOD
    CITY, PENNSYLVANIA), 1890-1910
HOUSTON PORCELAIN ENAMELING COMPANY (HO-
    POCO), HOUSTON, TEXAS*
IMPERIAL ENAMEL CO. LTD., NEW YORK, 1890-1910
INDUSTRIAL SIGNS INCORPORATED, 1940-1950
INGRAM-RICHARDSON, BEAVERFALLS, PA, 1901-1960
L. D. NELKE SIGNS, NEW YORK, 1900-1935
MARSH BROTHERS, TORONTO, ONTARIO, CANADA*
MARYLAND ENAMEL & SIGN CO., BALTIMORE, MARY-
    LAND, 1900-1920
MC MATH AXILROD, DALLAS, TEXAS, 1930-1965
MULHOLLAND, PHILADELPHIA, PA, 1925-1940
NATIONAL ENAMELING CO., CINCINNATI, OHIO,
    1895-1915

NESCO INC. SIGNS, NEW YORK & TOLEDO, OHIO*
ORME EVANS & CO. LTD., NEW YORK, 1895-1915
P & M, ORILLA, ONTARIO, CANADA, 1930-1950
PENNSYLVANIA ENAMEL, NEW CASTLE, PA*
PORCELAIN ENAMEL MANUFACTURING COMPANY,
    1910-1950
PORCELAIN METALS INCORPORATED, 1925-1950
RELIANCE ADVERTISING CO., NEW YORK, 1915-1930
SALES SERVICE CORPORATION, CHICAGO, ILLINOIS,
    1920-1930
SHANK SIGN CO., NEW YORK, 1920-1930
TENNESSEE ENAMEL MANUFACTURING CO., NASHVILLE,
    TENNESSEE, 1925-1970
TEXAS NEON ADVERTISING COMPANY, 1940-1950
TEXLITE, DALLAS, TEXAS, 1920-1960
VERIBRITE SIGNS, CHICAGO, ILLINOIS, 1915-1965
W. F. VILAS CO. LTD., COWANSVILLE, 1925-1950
WALKER & COMPANY, DETROIT, MI, 1925-1960
WESTERN ENAMELED STEEL SIGN COMPANY, CHICAGO,
    ILLINOIS
WOLVERINE PORCELAIN, DETROIT, MI, 1925-1945

Glossary

The following definitions are for words frequently encountered in collecting porcelain enamel advertising. The definitions may not be *Webster Dictionary* precise, as they are suited to the needs of our hobby.

Note: Pay special attention to the definitions of "reproduction" and "fantasy item." Except for the word "antique," "reproduction" is the most misused word in the English language!

BRACKET: A supporting device for a sign, normally made from flat and bar stock iron and constructed by hand.

BRUSH MARKS: The slight lines of fired-on frit that can be seen on many stenciled signs. These were the result of not brushing out all the area of a stencil.

BUTTON SIGN: Those signs that have the shape of a button, are circular and convex in form, but with a rolled-under perimeter, i.e. those round Coca-Cola signs of the 1940s and 1950s.

CLOISONNÉ: A multi-colored sign that uses metal partitions to separate colors. These are normally small advertising pieces such as emblems, badges, or buttons.

CORNER SIGN: Any sign designed to be displayed on the corner of a building by employing a special supporting bracket.

CRAZING: The appearance of fine cracks in the porcelain's finish. These will not have a uniform look, and are caused by the manufacturer not allowing proper cooling after running the sign through the kiln.

DECAL: The application of a lithographed paper to a sign's surface to be fired on. This was done in cases that proved too complicated for a silkscreen or stencil.

DIE-CUT: A shape or form that is cut with a die powered by a press. Any sign that is not square, rectangular, circular, or oval has a *die-cut* design by definition.

ETCHED: The loss of natural shine in porcelain. This is normally caused by chemicals in the atmosphere and/or by long-term exposure to a grounded surface.

EYELET: A single ring-like device, normally made of brass, that was pressed into the mounting hole openings. This offered protection to the porcelain on one side.

FANTASY ITEM: A privately produced advertisement that does not have any legitimately manufactured original counterpart with identical graphics and dimensions or structure.

FIRED: The process of heating metal and porcelain to the temperature required for fusing to occur, normally around 1600 degrees.

FLANGE: The area on a sign that is formed at ninety degrees to allow fastening to a wall.

FRIT: The vitreous material used to make porcelain enamel. Powder-like in consistency, it is pre-dyed with the appropriate color and will be fired in a kiln at approximately 1700 degrees Fahrenheit to produce a glass-like finish.

GRAPHICS: The artwork or design pattern on a sign.

GROMMET: A pair of washer-like rings, normally made of brass, that were designed to be pressed together as protection against chips from the mounting screws. These offered protection on both sides of a sign and were most often found on hanging type signs.

HUB CAP: A round convex sign.

INK STAMPED: A process of applying ink with a rubber stamp. The ink would be fired on in a kiln. Most commonly used to identify a manufacturer and address.

KILN: The high temperature furnace used to fire on porcelain.

LITHOGRAPHIC TRANSFER: Applying detailed images on porcelain by using a decal.

LOGO: The design or emblem used to represent a company's product or services. For example, the "gargoyle" was a logo used by Mobil Oil.

RE-ISSUE: A re-manufactured advertisement with the same graphics, dimensions, and structure as the original, and was produced by the original maker.

REPRODUCTION: A privately produced advertisement that has a legitimately manufactured original counterpart with identical graphics, dimensions, and structure.

ROLLED IRON: The process of "drawing" iron through a set of rollers to increase its strength. Mostly in use before steel could be made inexpensively.

SANS-SERIF: Lettering that is in "block" form.

SELF-FRAMED: Any sign that has a raised border to set off the design on the sign's inside.

SERIF: Lettering that has the ends made with a stylish flair.

SHELVING: Used to describe the effect of layering caused by successive layers of porcelain being fired one on top of the other. This will produce a "ridge" of porcelain at places where different colors border each other.

SILK SCREEN: A silk or synthetic mesh fabric used to apply frit to a sign's surface.

SPLIT FLANGE: A sign that was made with its ninety degree mounting done in two opposite directions.

STENCIL: A metallic sheet usually made of brass that was used to create lettering or a design. The intended pattern was cut out of the sheet, and this was placed on the sign's surface after frit was applied. The surface of the stencil was then brushed, eliminating the frit on the exposed cutout areas.

STRESS CRACKS: Hairline cracks in porcelain that are due to stresses created in use, most often from repeated battering by high winds.

STRIP SIGN: A sign that will measure considerably greater in width than height, long enough that the word "rectangle" does not describe its shape in the usual context.

VITRIFIED: To change into a glass-like substance by means of heat and fusion.

VOLCANO SCREW HOLE: The screw holes found in a sign that have a raised inner ridge. This design was patented by Ingram-Richardson in 1907.

Index